Art Movements and the Discourse of Acknowledgements and Distinctions

Themba Tsotsi

Vernon Series in Art

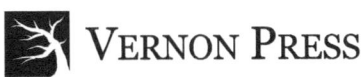

www.vernonpress.com

In the Americas:
Vernon Press
1000 N West Street,
Suite 1200, Wilmington,
Delaware 19801
United States

In the rest of the world:
Vernon Press
C/Sancti Espiritu 17,
Malaga, 29006
Spain

Vernon Series in Art

Library of Congress Control Number: 2016958913

ISBN: 978-1-62273-078-0

Table of Contents

The *Discourse* of Acknowledgments and *Distictions*: An Introduction

This is a work on the subject of critical theory. It incorporates the impact and role of visual art practice in cultural dispensation. The purpose of this introduction is to outline the methodology and provide some context.

The *discourse of acknowledgements and distinctions* introduces and makes extensive use of the following three key terms: *Hysteridence*, *Cerebrinity* and *Remembrance*. Hysteridence is the manner in which formative training even in diverse and separate communities has the same impact, is appropriated and disseminated in the same manner. Cerebrinity is the propensity for an individual to be freed by the knowledge he interacts with. In semiotics the 'sign' is comprised of not just a binary operation, it is also imbued with its own internal binary. Cerebrinity is the moment of understanding that the internal binary can be made compact or be illuminating. Remembrance is the recognition that symbolism in the physical structures of political leadership has communal, social, and historical significance. It is a conception of the city as a stage where we 'act' our significant roles in relationship with power structures.

This book is an installment in the oeuvre of the discourse of acknowledgements and distinctions. Two other books are planned on the discourse of acknowledgements and distinctions: "The Discourse of Acknowledgments and Distinctions" will be formal and longer and "Cerebrinity" will be a volume focused on the notion by the same name. The present book incorporates the above mentioned elements. It also argues that art participates and contributes to what is hysteridentical while engaging with what is moral.

The discourse in this installment expands on the notion of *hysteridence* as a facility that characterizes aspects of society. The discourse of critical theory has expanded on the semiotic significance of art, from Lyotard to psychoanalysts like *Jung*.

This work utilizes art to demonstrate the moral implications of the notion of hysteridence. Since hysteridence demonstrates the ambiguity of 'signs' in the context of modernity, it has implications for communities both in the lower and higher spectrum. The value of critical theory is that it examines the teleological implications of the didactic in the binary relationship between the symbolic power and the community.

Through art practice the inconsistencies in the binary relationship between the community and the symbolic power in the modern context can be discerned in the symbolic and the pragmatic structures.

The reason for incorporating psychoanalysis in this installment of the work is that it can demonstrate that hysteridence has existential connotations: 'being' has an independent relationship with 'signs', that through implicating towards the symbolic power also demonstrates that 'signs' in the social context and in the structures of modernity have the same moral implications.

Turner (1969) demonstrate how this binary has instituted *liminality* in the cultural dispensation as a condensation facility and imperative. He writes what he deems "communitas" in relation to the symbolic power. Turner's work is a quintessential example of the operation and presence of what is *hysteridentical* in the cultural dispensation. Writing from an anthropological perspective in the context of post-colonialism, he also postulates that societies that were colonized were and are influenced by western society in their traditions and rituals. He compares and equates the rituals and traditions of previously colonized communities with peripheral sociological communities in the western context. He characterizes both in the following manner:

> *"In their production we may catch glimpses of that unused evolutionary potential in mankind which has not yet been externalized and fixed in structure. Communitas breaks in through the interstices of structure, in liminality; at the edge of structure, in marginality; and from beneath structure, in inferiority. It is almost everywhere held to be sacred or 'holy', possibly because it transgresses or dissolves the norms that govern structured and institutionalized relationships and is accompanied by experiences of unprecedented potency. The processes of 'leveling' and*

> *'stripping', to which Goffman has drawn our at-*
> *tention, often appear to flood their subjects with*
> *affect. Instinctual energies are surely liberated*
> *by these processes, but I am now inclined to think*
> *that communitas is not solely the product of bio-*
> *logically inherited drives released from cultural*
> *constraints. Rather it is the product of peculiar*
> *human faculties, which include rationality, voli-*
> *tion and memory, and which develop with expe-*
> *rience of life in society." (Turner; 1969: 127-128)*

Turner emphasizes the condensation or metaphoric operation of the location of the margin in relation to the symbolic power, and how the relevant social strata are cognizant of their relationship with the symbolic power as passive and peripheral. The discourse of acknowledgments and distinctions seeks to demonstrate that the didactic implications in Turner's work concretize the logic of logocentrism as that which is the sole and primary source of formative and didactic sources.

It also highlights the teleological implication of art in the cultural dispensation as that which transcends what is affective, that it rather inculcates a spirit of community and collectivism that is organic and imbued with metonymic operations and the deconstructionist notion of infinite referral. It also demonstrates that what is hysteridentical has psychological connotations that are contingent on all strata of the cultural dispensation to be cognizant of how they are impacted by logocentrism and the respective passive and dominant locations in the relationship between the community and the symbolic power.

The work in this installment also seeks to demonstrate the measure with which 'signs' in the context of modernity operate with the condensation facility of the 'signifier'. The Victor Turner reference demonstrates the measure with which the significance of signification holds precedents over the operation of 'signs'. This can be demonstrated in art practice where 'signs' have to be imbued with transformational propensity or their epistemic implications in order for what is moral and metaphoric to be morally questioned.

He explicates that the notion of the 'communitas' emanates organically within the community, and is symbolic of aspects of the symbolic power that concretize the logic of 'absence' within the structure of the 'sign' of the community. When he talks about 'Instinctual energies' he is talking about what the discourse of acknowledgments and distinctions deems to be organic formative strategies that are influenced by the metonymic operation of 'signs'.

In the context of art practice these formative strategies are concretized for their metonymic implications, where their condensation aspects becomes 'transformed' and questioned for the psychological, cultural and sociological implications. Hysteridence also concretizes the metaphoric 'image' that emerges independent of the processes of the symbolic power to be that which concretizes the imperative role of art practice in the community and how the symbolic power cannot account for the fullest measure of presence.

That this 'image' is hysteridentical since it is 'defined' outside the context of symbolic power it is that which is loosely stratified or structured. In the context of art practice it can be characterized as 'positive' or positive in that it incorporates the didactic strategies of the symbolic power to differentiate 'itself' from 'itself' so that the artist can do the same. It can also be characterized as 'negative' since it emanates from the metaphoric 'absence' that characterizes community according to the processes of the symbolic power.

By incorporating art practice as a social aspect and demonstrating the role of signification the work can demonstrate the measure with which notions such as 'communitas' or 'liminality' are that which cannot be identified in the cultural dispensation. Since within the binary relationship between the community and the symbolic power critical theory has demonstrated that both are influenced and are contingent on the epistemic logic of the initium or what Foucault (1969) has designated as the enunciative field, where 'signs' can be accessed and utilized either for condensation or metonymic implications.

This installment in the discourse of acknowledgments and distinctions seeks to demonstrate the measure with which art primarily engages the metonymic in the operation of the 'sign'. It also seeks to demonstrate the measure with which the symbolic power operates primarily as the maternal aspect in the cultural dispensation. It will also demonstrate how psycho-analyses demonstrate the deconstructionist notion of infinite referral in the structural operations of 'signs'.

An Attempt at Critical Structures

The installment focuses on visual art practice for a number of reasons. One is to examine the 'nature' of 'signification' in the cultural dispensation, that location where the community and the symbolic power are contingent on the initium in order to access their relationship to 'signs'. Two: The work has incorporated psychoanalysis, this is consistent with the aspect of critical theory where the work examines the society through a normative lens. Three: The work has also incorporated the work of critical theory or cultural theory oeuvre with notions of figures like Lyortard, Baudrillard, Spivak and Derrida. Through the lens of writers like Hegarty, Morton, who have outlined and explicated critical theory for those who have a secondary access to it. Their works also concretize the goals of critical theory to make their concepts accessible to a larger and broader reading spectrum, where the intended academic goals and implicit symbolic presence of the work can be recognized.

Four: The work examines the goals and role of visual art practice in context of modernity, with interests in the context post colonialism or advanced capitalism. Examining the historic significance of art movements like Dadaism (http://www.theart-story.org/ movement-dada.htm) and Resistance art of the Black Consciousness Movement (http://www.contemporary-african-art.com/resistance-art.html) (1968-1971) here in South Africa. Through the works of artists like Tristan Tzara, Hugo Ball and Marcell Duchamp. Through their production of works that utilize the cultural impact of the ready made or found object in their works, the movement discoursed the impact of conscription during the wars and the fallibility of identity in western society through the symbolism that the found object afforded.

Resistance art in South Africa through the works of artists like William Kentridge, Sue Williamson, Helen Sibidi and Willem Bester. Artists that are still relevant in the contemporary art scene in South Africa and around the world. The work will then be able to draw a comparison between art practice in the context of modernity with the intention of demonstrating that art is conscious of the 'absence' that informs the community. It is an 'absence' whose agency is informed by anarchism as a moral force than a reactionary violent strategy on the part of the community to demonstrate it is imbued with agency.

Both movements are consistent with the aspect in the methodology of a critical theory where it has to demonstrate how 'being' is conscious of his or her "emancipation" in the cultural dispensation, where one has the "epistemic tools necessary to make one free—to change the world and the structure of governing social relations in ways that increase one's ability to live and develop freely" (Little: http://understandingsociety.blogspot.co.za/2013/03/critical-theory-in-frankfurt-school.html).

Through the discourse of acknowledgements and distinctions and its notion of hysteridence the work has included and subsumed the limitations and freedom of language. Where deconstructionism calls for 'invention' of words, it is consistent with critical theory when it talks about the limitations of language instigating a measure of observing the world that attempts to be objective but is rather is subjective due to nature of objectivity being a "linguistic construction" that "privileges the objective label" (http://www.qualres.org/HomeCrit-3518.html).

Mbembe (2001) demonstrates how objectivity is privileged in the cultural dispensation and enables 'being' to be conscious of their emancipation or their implication towards the symbolic power. In his discourse he talks about the notion of "'*displacement*' is not only intended to signify dislocation, transit or the impossibility of any centrality other than one that is provisional" (2001:15) it is also as the notion of hysteridence seeks to inculcate that which concretizes subjectivity in the context of modernity.

The term hysteridence is an interpretive facility that helps the discourse explicate that the cultural dispensation has be subjected to unifying 'negative' and 'positive' didactic or formative strategies that are relevant in affluent community to the same ethical extent non-affluent communities. That these ethics have economic, social, universal, psychological and existential implications.

Mbembe not only discourses the measure with which the question of origins in the context of modernity are not just tenuous and temporary, he also discourses their overt existential connotations. Through the facility of implication towards the symbolic power or the facility of the 'initio', 'being' has to be cognizant of the measure with which modernity is contingent on structures of signification than the operation of 'signs'. Mbembe demonstrates that 'being' is conscious of the historical epoch in which he resides, this not only makes him or her conscious of the structures of signification, but he also demonstrates how subjectivity necessitates 'alternative' formative strategies 'formulated' in the organic context of the community.

For the writer it becomes significant in the critical theory to incorporate his or her social experience. This has connotations for his or her linguistic limitations and guidelines; it also has connotations for recognizing the social context for reliance on the 'signifying' processes of 'signs' rather than the operation of the 'sign'. It may appear that this does not have any methodological or theoretical substance, since the critical theory espouses individual emancipation in the cultural dispensation, the writer can safely state that through his experience of the social intercourse through its overtly repetitive structure. His perception of the social context is consistent with critical theory where methods combine "observation and interviewing with approaches that foster conversation and reflection" (http://www.qualres.org/ HomeCrit-3518.html).

In this installment this facility is provided by the facility of visual art to not only endure over a period of time or through historical epochs, also through art's propensity to instigate cultural discourse or moral discourse. The work seeks to able to demonstrate the didactic imperative in the cultural dispensation is rendered stable and concrete operating without the fluid epistemic connotations of the context prior the substitution into modernity.

The installment seeks to be also able to demonstrate the measure with which 'signs' able to emancipate themselves as critical theory states is necessary in order for a critical theory to be effective. The emphasis on the psychological impact and implication of hysteridence the work seeks to demonstrate the significance of observation in the context of modernity. That observation concretizes the logic of the 'pure' or 'essentialist'. Through psycho-analyses is able to discourse and problematize the logic of the 'pure' or essentialist notion, where the epistemic has connotations for ontological.

The notion of hysteridence seeks to demonstrate the measure the contingency of observation concretizes the epistemic implications of agency in 'being'. That through the social facility of the artist this epistemic contingency still has relevance to 'being' drives.

Chapter 1

Art Movements and Distinctions

In this chapter the discourse will explicate the notion of hysteridence through Stuart Hall's notion of 'encoding and decoding'. Vasiliev, who explicates Hall's notion, demonstrates the essentialism with which 'signs' in the context of modernity operate with in order to differentiate social, cultural and economic backgrounds. Like what is hysteridentical the discourse how in the context of modernity 'signs' are influenced by a symbiotic relationship, that can be detected to be operational in their respective 'oppositional' location between communities in higher strata and in the lower strata of society.

The chapter will also discourse how in the context of the substitution aesthetics were discoursed with formative implications. It will demonstrate how this strategy concretizes the measure with which the symbolic power differentiated the operation of 'signs' in the rural or feudal context to the context of modernity.

The discourse will demonstrate how the social context is imbued with a metaphysical element that enables the logic of 'absence' in the structure of the social transaction that necessitates discursive training. The discourse will also demonstrate how this metaphysical aspect in the cultural dispensation influences the measure with which art is produced and how art formulates discourse. That formulation in the context of art has teleological relations with the symbolic power that concretize an originary relationship between the community and the supplement independent of the symbolic power.

That 'being' has to implicate towards the symbolic power, art movements demonstrate that this implication has relevance for the originary aspect in 'being' that has a relationship with the supplement. Art movements also operate with a supplementary aspect, when they are cognizant of the manner in which they have to implicate towards the institutions and their commercial ethics of advanced capitalism.

The chapter will also demonstrate how through the hysteri-dentical operation of the notion of the 'initio' and the 'absence' that informs the context of the community, there is a metaphysical implication in the context of the symbolic power that relies on 'being' to implicate towards the symbolic power. That 'being' and the object have to be cognizant of their implicating towards the symbolic power to be that which concretizes their location in relation to the formulaic processes of the symbolic power.

The discourse will also demonstrate how 'signs', 'being' and the social context are not provided with a facility to juxtapose due to them being 'ends' unto themselves or the symbolic power inculcating that they are not influenced by the notion of the trace. It will seek to demonstrate the measure with which the 'object' in the context of art through the symbolic power's conception of presence/'presence' is able to incite discourse about the fullest measure of presence. That through accretion that is in necessary in the operation of the 'sign', demonstrate how 'meaning' is never stable but is in constant flux.

Art Movements and Distinctions

Postcolonial conditions and the contexts upon which art reflects are based on the disruptive histories of previously colonized people. They can be characterized as that which is hysteridentical according to the discourse of acknowledgements and distinctions. In that postcolonial art emanates from the negative myths about colonized peoples that were propagated by the symbolic power. It is art that instigated or was influenced by social political movements that resulted in the movements and the art itself being curtailed by the jurisdiction of the symbolic power.

Dadaism for example also emanates from this similar context and is inspired by the measure of the negative that characterized mid 20th century volatility. It was an art movement that was reactionary to the universal conscription that was taking place in the cultural dispensation. What enables Dadaism to be characterized as hysteridentical is the fact that at its inception it was informed by the ambiguity of that which it was reactionary towards. This included the communal or existential ethics of self-expression that conscription and the war imposed on individuals.

The value of art practice is that it can enable the community to exalt discourse to a level of morality that is about the contemporary than about history or the future. This is also part of what informs the notion of hysteridence in that it is a notion that is concretized by the measure of the contemporary that negotiates the relationship between the community and the symbolic power. In that the measure with which individuality is formalized in the context of advanced capitalism is based on that which is unfolding in the structure of the 'initio' and what is transpiring outside of one. What is formative and didactic in advance capitalism is peripheral to the extent that what is originary about cultural and individual didactic principles has been inculcated in the impersonal formative training that is riddled with the despotism of the jurisdiction of power.

Hysteridence in art practice is concretized by the fact that it is imbued with the measure of an organic jurisdiction that operates beyond advance capitalism's formative training. It is also informed by the initium or the facet in 'signs' that operates as the supplementary. This can be exemplified in Dadaism by the use of colloquialisms and the 'value' of the object as more than just a consumerist utility, and is symbolic of the immediacy and transience that characterizes the cultural dispensation and relegates the ontological to the periphery of the symbolic power formative training.

It can also be exemplified by Hall's system as explicated in Vasiliev (2015: http://www.evasilev.com/blog/notes-on-stuart-hall-encoding-decoding) of "encoding and decoding". It is a conception that examines the structure of the 'signs' of representations and their cultural source. Just like art practice television as a social institution is contingent on communal perception for teleological justification, where what is negative and positive can be detected to be imbued with a didactic and symbiotic relationship. The system demonstrates how the community is cognizant of the 'signs' of representation and their external source, which concretizes what is hysteridenctical and the 'absent' structure of the 'sign' through what Hall calls (Vasiliev, 2015) "polysemy" the propensity of the 'sign' to reference its meaning towards the system which conceived and concretizes its limits.

Another value of art is that it places the ontological parallel to the formative training of the cultural dispensation as that which is imbued with the discourse of the originary. That the traditional cultural training has sought to demonstrate is part of the ontological shortcomings of the cultural dispensation in the context of transition or substitution from the rural to the urban context.

Art practice demonstrates that the substitution was or that concretizes the jurisdiction or power of the symbolic power as that which places a severing mechanism between the two contexts. That the substitution discourses aesthetics as a formative tool when 'being' is conscious of them in relation to the pre-colonial and feudal context. This formative implication is also relevant when individuals imbued with the 'initio' seek to justify their jurisdiction in a social context. In that the jurisdiction is not only a disassociation tool between advance capitalism and the rural or feudal context. It is also that which renders the notion of aesthetics in relation to capitalism and its training as that which operate with the presence of 'non-presence' in the cognitive space and the structure of 'signs' as a result of traditional cultural training.

Deconstructionism is a discourse that has demonstrated that 'signs' or means of inculcating the traditional cultural training are that which are imbued with an ambiguity that is characterized by what is metaphysical and is imbued with the despotism of the logocentric. Hysteridence seeks to demonstrate that what is metaphysical is also that which exhibits that what is ontological in the context of advance capitalism is imbued with the immediacy of the social context. That this concretizes a measure of this negative 'absence' being devoid of the facility of the 'initio' that subjugates and enables implication towards the symbolic power. This becomes pronounced in the encounter between the citizen and the public administrator, where the jurisdiction of power imbues the 'being' with the 'initio' with a negative 'presence' that logocentrism concretizes as that which is fundamental to the logical administering of the ethics of advance capitalism.

What is originary in 'being', outside the institutions of the symbolic power and without the didactic paradigms that characterized their formative training, 'being' in the social immediacy has to assume a 'presence' of cultural training. Hysteridence states this is acquired and manifests through the combination of appropriation and repetition in the social context. That the ephemeral, transcendental cognitive and transformational manifestation of the art production, is also imbued with the metaphysical connotations of the social context that is contradictory to traditional cultural training. That incorporated in the art production is also the originary connotations of self-expression and cultural appropriation that was fundamental to archaic Man.

That the art production imbues the cognitive with the immediate operation of the principles of condensation and displacement that are fundamental to the existential 'possession' of the 'initio' in the context of cultural training. In the Dadaism artistic movement, there was a clear acknowledgement of the cultural dispensation being 'conscious' of the measure of plethora of 'signs' in the cultural dispensation as that which are part of the discourse and politics of the cultural dispensation.

The art movement seeks to demonstrate that the symbolic power had already concretized the measure of formative training that makes it incumbent on the 'being' to self implicate to the symbolic power. Hysteridence is a notion that purports that to self implicate to the symbolic power requires what is originary in 'being' therefore that is not imbued with traditional social training. That this is what the cultural dispensation makes clear upon the individual through the inculcation of the 'initio'.

The measure with which is imbued with the measure of the 'initio' parallel to the originary cultural 'location' precipitates the discourse and drama of aesthetics in the context of advance capitalism. The art movement is hysteridentical in that the cognitive existential space when it appropriates the metaphoric or condensation facility of advanced capitalism which is the 'initio', it becomes embroiled in the measure of 'absence' that characterizes 'being' prior to the traditional social training.

Art movements rely on the condensation facility in the structure of the 'sign'. It not only demonstrates a relationship between the context of advance capitalism and the feudal or rural context. It also exhibits that 'signs' are that which still operate in the structure of that which the discourse of acknowledgments and distinctions designates as the initium, or that loosely stratified context that 'signs' operate in. The initium is different from Foucault's notion of the 'enunciative field' in the context of the cultural dispensation. In that it subsumes the transformational nature of 'signs' or that which can be characterized as the displacement or metonymic operation of the 'sign'. Foucault demonstrates that the enunciative field is incorporated in the formulation or manufacturing of the discursive itself, it is also that which supplements the notion of the discursive through the evidence of incorporating 'signs' as that which have been and are utilized in the social and institutional contexts of the cultural dispensation. For Foucault these 'signs' are that which incorporate the facility of the logocentric, not only as intrinsic to the measure of what is metaphysical about the 'initio', but also to concretize the 'absence' of implicating without the traditional social training.

Art movements and art practice are that which imbue what is metaphoric or the condensation facility in the 'sign' with the measure of repetition, a measure of the transformational, and a measure of the anachronistic. More significantly even in art practice there is a measure of immediacy in the piece that has implication for 'presence' and presence in the cultural institutions that administer art. Though art movements are cognizant of the logic that they have to establish a relationship with institutions, this not only concretize the art movement and the cultural institution to the notions of the supplementary and the supplement, it is at the ethic and logic of the commodity that enables the art piece to operate as a 'durable' or 'fluctuating' commodity in terms of its value. That this has implications for its existential symbolic connotations as much as its condensation facility as a cultural product.

Art practice and art movements are that which demonstrate that 'being' with his or her originary identity connotations, in order to operate in the paradigm and logic of the supplementary and the supplement has to be imbued with a condensation facility of 'possession' in order to be incorporated in a particular cultural dispensation. That this not only has implications for that which is metaphysical about community or even the ubiquity that characterizes the cultural dispensation. It is also that which exhibits the measure of immediacy in the cultural dispensation subsumes a measure of 'absence' of power and the transient politics of control that the traditional social trainings imbues the facility of the jurisdiction of the 'initio' with.

That art not only provides a contemporary symbolic or metaphoric facility for the audience, but that if one is cognizant of the accretion facility of the initium, then one is also cognizant of the originary connotations that a condensation or metaphoric facility is imbued with. That a condensation facility is imbued with formative or didactic facilities, originary connotations, supplementary connotations through accretion facility in the 'sign'. It is also that which is metaphysical and transcendental in that the condensation facility enables the 'signs' to be imbued with logocentric connotations.

The artist though relies on the originary operation of the condensation facility not only as that which is formative but has connotations for a relationship with the supplement and therefore the collective unconscious. That this is the measure of the 'sign' that de-constructionism states operates with phenomenological connotations that imbue a 'sign' as that which 'is' or infinite referral. In the context of art production and the visual vocabulary that art movements and artists have at their disposal, the 'sign' is barren of the measure to 'coincide with itself' in that it has already been 'defined'. Bearing the role of the supplement in mind, it operates as that which 'is'. If we take the Dadaist proverbial example of the urinal, even though a urinal is a product of advance capitalism, the immediacy of the social context without the originary connotations of the biological activity that is associated with the utility, there is imbedded the measure of the condensation and displacement in the 'invention' of the implement. There is also a measure of the necessary physical jurisdiction that in the context of advance capitalism is imbued with power. As a formative training tool the urinal in the context of the art movement and its philosophy that is partly inspired by what is existential. It is about the fundamentals being devoid of what is political but incorporates history in terms of the propensity of the 'sign' to accrue meaning. In the context of the 'sign' history has to necessarily be imbued with a measure of the philological in that in order for the utility of the urinal to be imbued with transformational connotations it has to have been 'defined' in relation to the pragmatism of the utility but also to the originary and symbolic activity of the biological task that an urinal is used for.

This is not only a facility that is enabled by accretion it is also a facility that enables the art work to induce a discourse about the course that the cultural dispensation is taking after the advent of the substitutions in the period that is generally characterized as the development of advance capitalism. The art movement seeks to engage and discourse the measure in the in the 'sign' in its operation in the global cultural dispensation as that which is imbued with a universal and related to the notion of the supplementary or the initium.

The difference between the initium and the supplementary is that the supplementary in the structure of the 'sign' enables the 'sign' to operate with the measure of the originary logic that the supplementary operation of the 'sign' imbues it with the propensity to multifaceted that it not only operates with the essentialism that logocentrism inculcates. The supplementary in the 'sign' is also that which is about concretizing the image of the originary as that which is universal, it is also about the measure of the 'sign' to account for fullest measure of presence that is not just about a single cultural designation. The initium on the other hand according to this discourse is symbolic of the accretion that in the production of the discursive and is necessary in the articulation of the supplementary in the context and didactic role of aesthetics.

Not only is this the measure with which the philological is logical accretion it is also the measure with which the cultural dispensation is able to imbue that which is metaphoric with transformational propensities. This enables the purposes of appropriation but it is also the measure with which the supplementary operates as more than that which is symbolic. It becomes incorporated in that which is practical about didactic and formative strategies of the cultural dispensation.

The initium is not that which accounts for fullest measure of presence, but like art practice is 'responsible' for the measure in the cultural dispensation that can exhibit the measure with which 'sign' relates and accrues meaning between relationships.

Art, Presence/'presence' and Juxtaposition

The fact that art practice has had to be imbued with a global communication and interaction context is not only related to the measure of economic and democratic exchange, rather it has implications for a global ethic that the notion of hysteridence states is part of the universal character of advance capitalism. In that hysteridence is not only about how what is formative and didactic has been accrued in the cultural dispensation. It is also about the universal humanistic ethic that is implicit in the economic ethics that characterize advance capitalism.

Imbedded in the originary production of art, there is an ambiguity that is about the transformational propensity of the 'sign' and its relationship to what is pragmatic about the operation of the initium or the enunciative field that is a harbinger of meaning for 'signs'. Not only is this about the measure of the 'sign' being related to what is originary it is also the means with which what is didactic in a particular epoch can be gauged to be didactically relevant and gauged whether it is related to the supplement. In that the art production through the transformational propensity of a 'sign' enables the 'sign' to 'temporarily' operate beyond both the influence of the supplementary, the initium and the enunciative field. This not only demonstrates the measure of the artist or 'being' to be imbued with metaphysical propensities, it also demonstrates that the 'sign' or the object are that which exhibit the measure of 'presence' and 'non-presence' that what is metaphysical that the traditional social training states is imbedded in the transience of the immediacy in the social context.

In the social context according to traditional social training the 'object' and 'being' are that which are involved through self-implication in their existential or originary or organic implications. These are about identity formation and what is metaphysical about the object. That presence relies on the 'being' to be able to witness and the object to be essentialist and pure without being tarnished by residual previous experience. That there is another form of 'presence' that is about what is metaphysical through the legitimacy of logocentrism and concretizes that 'being' and the object are that which are an 'end' unto themselves in terms of implication to the symbolic power and being inculcated as cultural 'signs' with didactic relevance respectively.

Traditional social training, states that what is phenomenological about a 'sign' is self-referential and related to auto affection in relation to 'being' respectively. This does not enable them juxtaposition due to the transience of the immediacy of the social interaction. The art object through both the medium of the artist and the artifact itself, enable juxtaposition that is primarily symbolic due to the transformational propensity of 'signs' operating as condensation or metaphoric facilities instead of displacement or metonymic connotations. That this is related to the measure of art practice engaging that which is moral, ethical, and teleological in the relationship between 'being' and objects or utilities. That the relationship between 'being' and what the symbolic power's traditional social training inculcates is related to the context of the substitution instead of what is accrued about sovereignty. The art production seeks to engage the measure in the object that demonstrates that what is epistemic also has implications for the community and accretion. That the transience of the exhausted social interaction in the context of advanced capitalism purports that the moment exhausts itself instead of being juxtaposed.

Presence or 'presence' in the context of the art production is about the measure of the future as that which imbues the notion of 'meaning' as that which enables the art production to be inundated with value. That it is also as that which enables it to function symbolically in the future as well as the present. That the art object is about illuminating the 'now' of the general social context when it is about consciousness and it is about existential relevance when it is about what is symbolic about the unconscious. That in art practice the 'meaning' of an object is never that which is stable it is rather that which has to fluctuate. This is not only the character of advanced capitalism, it is also the measure with which deconstructionism demonstrates that 'moments' are always that which are in constant flux.

The artifact is the quintessential example of this in that even though what is symbolic about it is static through the form of the piece and through the limitations of the canvas, it is also that which has implications for the future and the propensity for the 'sign' to operate as that which 'is' or to extend 'meaning'.

That the artifact's value can also emanate from its quintessential measure to relate or be relatable, where it can cease to be about power and demonstrate that the measure of the 'now' is not that which is solely contingent on the auto-equation or the auto-referential propensity of the object and 'being' respectively. It is also that which engages the cultural dispensation through the accretion that is imbedded in the object and the discourse of history.

In that the discourse of history implicitly or overtly engages implications of the future both in terms of aesthetics and their formative didactic connotations. It is also the measure with which demonstrates that the subject of the piece engages with the substitutions' notions of the fullest measure of presence.

Art practice is the only social 'institution' that has implications that can account for diversity in the cultural dispensation, that this is the measure that connects its discourse to the impact of accretion for and from the facility of collective unconscious as that which demonstrates that a 'signs' 'meaning' is never stable but through accretion is constantly in flux.

What is existential about producing art is that it is a manifestation that demonstrates that a divisibility of 'being' or 'self' in the relationship between 'being' and the object is necessary and enables 'meaning' to be that which 'is' instead of being confined to that which is essentialist and pure in the structure of a 'sign'. The artifact cannot account for the fullest measure of the social context, the discourse of acknowledgements and distinctions seeks to demonstrate that the necessary divisibility between 'being', context and the object demonstrates that 'moments' are not exhausted but becomes appropriated and incorporated in the plethora of 'signs' in the unconscious. That this also becomes embroiled in the propensity in 'being' to be conscious of the residual past experience and the implications of the future.

In that the primary and teleological implications of the artifact are to engage and discourse subjects that have connotations for that which is 'outside' of the subject itself. That it also has to be informed by the subject in a manner that exhibits that the subject is not static or simply related to the auto-referential discourse of the art production. In the art production the 'self' becomes embroiled in the discourse of 'presence/absence' that imbues 'being' and the social circumstances he or she is informed by with metaphysical connotations. That a measure in the discourse of the artifact has to be imbued with metaphysical connotations in that it engages the 'absence' of the past and future 'meanings' of both the discourse and the object, but it also includes the measure of 'being' as that which 'is'.

The measure of 'being' in the context of producing art is also that which demonstrates the extent to which 'being' is ephemeral and metaphysical. In that in the context of producing art 'being is imbued with the measure of the essentialism or what is originary about self-expression. "Being" is also that which demonstrates that 'being' is the facility or medium that imbues object with its transformational propensities. That since the artist and the audience are conscious of this transformational penchant they are also that which enable the art work to incite discourse. The critique of the nature of the metaphysical in the discourse of deconstructionism is partly established on the notion that questions the measure of the 'sign' to be essentialist and pure, without the external influence of residual past 'meanings' of a 'sign'. When this is compared with the context of cultural production and 'being' creative expression, the artist can demonstrate the measure of 'absence' or possible future in the structure of a 'sign'. That this essentialist structure in 'signs' is also the measure with which logocentrism's the notion of the metaphysical in the traditional social training that states that there is an 'absence' of the logic and ethics of the symbolic power in 'being'.

The discourse also seeks to state that the 'sign' or what is teleological about art is not that which is critiqued by the traditional training's notion of the metaphysical, rather it is what is utilitarian or symbolic about art that the symbolic power questions. That these grounds are based on the notion of 'signs' in the cultural dispensation being structured by what is essentialist and pure. That this notion of the 'sign' between the cultural production and the traditional notions of the 'sign' according to modernity, is what enables there to be an 'accident' between the symbolic power and the production of the art.

Not only does this articulate and outline what is hysteridentical but it is also that which demonstrates that form and what is formulaic about the symbolic power's policies are both informed by this measure of the metaphysical in the 'sign'. That is about articulating what is teleological about art production and communal cohesion respectively. That they both operate on the abstract and metaphysical arena, they are that which discourse the measure of 'presence' and 'absence' that the foundations of modernity are based on and that concretize the location of jurisdiction of power in community being contingent on the symbolic power.

If we consider what is reactionary about art, it primarily operates on the political or social consciousness arena, and that this is the measure with which it interrogates notions of 'presence' in the structure of the 'sign'. This is where art can interrogate the measure of the teleological, the measure of the epistemic, the philological and the extent to which the 'sign' has accrued and relinquished 'meaning' in the context of its use in the enunciative field and in the context of what this discourse designates as the initium.

Presence in the context of art is ablative in that it connects the 'presence' in the structure of the object, it is also that which enables the 'being' with his originary power to imbue and render an object with transformational propensities. That it is also the measure which concretizes 'presence' to be teleological and epistemic. In order for them to be relevant there has to be a measure of creativity, that articulates and concretizes the veracity of both the context and the veracity of the discourse. In that 'presence' is made palpable by context, that space where language concretizes the relationship between the discourse, the object and the supplement, in that not only does this demonstrate a relationship with the symbolic power, it also that which can exhibit the propensity of the artwork to be moral, philosophical or be imbued with historic connotations.

'Presence' is also that which demonstrates that the object has a relationship with the logocentric logic that venerates what is epistemic and what is essentialist about an object. Art reveals that what enables an object or discourse to be transformational is 'presence' itself, even when this 'presence' is 'absent'. In the measure of the hysteridentical this is also the means with which the drama that is inherent between the community and the symbolic power discourse 'presence' as that which is 'present' through the facility of particular conditions that can be demonstrated are not essential in the formative and didactic implications for 'being' but are informed by the measure of the 'initio'.

Since the 'initio' is abstract but is imbued with the structure of the 'pure' and the 'essentialist', it comes to form part of the form of the art-work and the narratives or formulations that the artist deems to be relevant.

What articulates what is hysteridentical about this context is that the artist is conscious of the contemporary notions of definitions of the 'sign' or object, that this is also the measure with which he or she can interrogate the measure of 'presence' and the essentialist logic of logocentrism.

This way what is teleological about the structure of the 'sign' can be discoursed for both its supplementary measures and its relationship to the supplement. That 'presence' has ontological implications where and when it can exhibit the propensity to relate or sustain a relationship. In that in this context 'presence' is becomes imbued with notions of power, power according to the discourse of acknowledgements and distinctions   enables the interrogation of the binaries. In that in order for a binary to be concretized art production can demonstrate that there has to be a 'presence' in the structure of the object or discourse that is an anti-thesis of the dominant structure of the symbolic power.

In the context of the art production both the artist and the object are imbued with a measure of a teleological 'presence' that is originary and operates beyond the measure and logic of the logocentric. That this is the measure with which they interrogate the measure of the 'absence' in the cultural dispensation or discourse that is not just about power between 'being' and the symbolic power. Which can be about the measure of exigency and what is moral between the symbolic power and the community.

Since art can address an exigency it is about how 'presence' implicitly operates with a measure of 'absence' between the community and the symbolic power. That even though what is symbolic about this relationship the community is cognizant of, it is also that which exhibits that what is symbolic is not just related to the logocentric notion of 'presence' but it is imbued with a measure of the metaphysical. Since this metaphysical penchant is contemporary, art production and discourse exhibits that 'presence' is concretized as teleological when it is allowed to be transformational.

This is also the measure that influenced the context of the ablative exercise of the substitution from the rural to the urban context or paradigm of modernity. The contingency of art on 'signs' makes the clear the ambiguity that is inherent in the operations of an object. That art works with the locations in the structure of the 'sign' that are symbolic and pragmatic or inculcated in the cultural dispensation. That this ambiguity allows the 'sign' to be transformational, and to have implications that are imbued with the contemporary, the historic and also the future. That the ambiguity is also that which allows the 'sign' to be imbued with the measure of the 'possibility of the future' that space where what is phenomenological about a 'sign' is not just limited to the contemporary operations of the 'sign' but is also related to the measure that demonstrates that 'being' and individuality are related to what is supplementary and the supplement.

In that 'presence' is not just about the measure in the 'sign' that demonstrates that the current epoch is cognizant of that which is epistemic in the 'sign'. This is not only to articulate what is philosophical or teleological about the measure of the 'sign' to operate, it is also about the propensity of the 'sign' to demonstrate that there is a measure of infinite referral within the structure of the 'sign'. That part of the operations of art production are to exhibit this, that it is also that which is imperative to the existential implications of art production, that through the cultural production and the operation of a particular 'sign' are that which can discourse the measure of self-implicating to the symbolic power.

Art is a practice seeks to demonstrate that implicating towards the symbolic power is not about conflict, that even though there is a measure of the originary in the structure of the binary between the symbolic power and the community. Since art is about expression, art is able to demonstrate that what is didactic in the binary becomes embroiled in the discourse of the exhausted and immediate social experience.

Longevity in the art-work is part of the discourse of the art work, it is also that which is about the measure in the cultural dispensation that operates with what is utilitarian about an art object. That which concretizes the measure of the binary between 'being' and the symbolic power. Since the artifact is defined as an object or is durable, 'being' who produces the object occupies the location of the metaphysical, in that not only does the 'object' become imbued with a mystical 'meaning', it is also that which exhibits that the notion of differance seeks to demonstrate what is transcendental about the relationship between objects and 'being'.

The notion of the transcendental or differance is also that which discourses the measure of 'absence' in the structure of the 'sign' but also in the structure of the binary or dichotomy in the relationship between 'being' and the symbolic power.

That 'absence' is that measure in the structure of the relationship that can exhibit that power is contingent on both the locations of the binary. That even though what defines it as conflict is contingent on conceptions of the originary it is also that which is about how what is epistemic in the dominant location of the binary articulates what is epistemic in the relationship between 'being' and the symbolic power. That the implications of the future in the relationship between the symbolic power and the 'sign' are that which can demonstrate that 'absence' is the measure with which the dominant location in the dichotomy in the relationship between the community and the symbolic power it is validated by.

In that the measure of the future in the structure of the 'sign' and the 'meanings' it has accrued throughout its originary history are that which can demonstrate the operation of the supplementary in the 'sign' 'comprises' this sense of the 'absence'. It is significant that this measure of the 'absence' is described as an adjective in that a supplementary can articulate both what is transformational but also this sense of the ablative in the structure of the 'sign' especially in the context of a substitution. Art production can be characterized as a mini substitution, in that not only does it exhibit the measure of 'signs' to transform within a particular epoch it also demonstrates the measure with which a 'sign' can have its own supplementary aspect.

The supplementary aspect of the 'sign' in the structure of a 'sign' is able to exhibit the measure with which an audience and the artist can be distant from the relationship between the 'sign' and the supplement. In that when the 'sign' interacts or operates it is unable to cater for the fullest measure of presence in a particular epoch. When it is 'new' or without the tyranny of a cultural definition it is related to the fullest measure of presence through the virtue of its 'presence' of the 'absence' of 'meaning'. The virtue of 'presence' in the context of an object upon the first encounter is ephemeral, mysterious and transient. That what is supplementary is defined by the acknowledgement of an 'absence' from the clutches of a cultural category.

Art can demonstrate that an object or 'sign' has at its originary disposal a facility for accretion that is about always already established relationships. This is also the measure of the transformational. It also exhibits clearly the representational measure with which 'being' and cultural formulations imbue on a 'sign', represents the measure with which 'being' and the community are also imbued with the originary measure of the supplementary.

What becomes operational in the context of 'being' in order to demonstrate the measure of the metaphysical and the measure of independence of the 'sign'? Notions of power and representation become embroiled in the discourse of the transformational and the relationship it induces through other 'signs' or facilities of transformation.

In the context of art 'being' is the overt facility for transformation, 'being' is also the metaphysical facility for the teleological measure of the 'sign' and of the production of art itself. The measure of the substitution is not that which is defined by desire rather it is defined by expression, creative or cultural, that it is also about the measure of 'absence' that can induce satisfaction or fulfillment through auto-affection. Since art is about that which is transformational, it is about the measure that is about articulating the fullest measure of accretion and 'presence' in the structure of the 'sign', which can include discourse about 'future' conceptions of a 'sign' in the cultural dispensation.

If the measure of 'absence' is not considered then the fullest measure of accretion will not include the measure of accretion prior to the 'sign's interaction with 'being' or the cultural category. Rather it will imbue it with modernity's notion of essentialism and purity that concretizes the measure of the binary in the structure of the 'sign'.

Chapter 2

Art and Cerebrinity

This chapter seeks to demonstrate the measure with which the production of art is tantamount to the production of knowledge. Part of the significance of critical theory is that it interrogates the subjectivity that is operational in the production of the discursive. In this chapter the work seeks to demonstrate the measure with which art practice discourses the capacity of 'signs' in the context of modernity to imbue certain 'signs' with formative connotations and 'other' 'signs' that are deemed to be 'lacking' formative implications.

By exhibiting the necessary reconciliation between the conscious and the unconscious, and the facility in art practice that espouses the deconstructionist notion of infinite deferral or differance. That this applies to being conscious of the role of the unconscious in everyday experiences as facilitating the liberating impact of desire for that which is didactic.

The chapter will demonstrate the measure with which the art practice induces a cerebrinous experience, and the extent to which they both have connotations for a metaphysical experience, by exhibiting the measure with which cerebrinity is comprised of social, intellectual and pragmatic implications.

In order to concretize the role of the metaphysical in the social context, the discourse will demonstrate the measure with which it is significant to master social contexts in the vein of the master archetype. This is necessary due to the social context in the context of the community being 'barren' of formative and didactic implications. To master social contexts, is also a demonstration of the measure of self-implicating towards the symbolic power.

The chapter will also discourse how the rise of art movements like Dadaism concretized the measure with which the metaphysical and materialist values were questioned. That the art movement was able to exhibit the fragmented nature of the cultural formulation in the processes of the symbolic power, how in the context of the First World War, the 'image' of plenitude that characterized the cultural dispensation, disintegrated. Dadaism was able to exhibit how it was incumbent on the community to implicate both towards the symbolic power and to master the social context.

Of Art and Cerebrinity

Cerebrinity according to the discourse of acknowledgements and distinctions is the intellectual process of illumination in the context of an encounter with knowledge. In the context of art this measure of illumination can be characterized as an unbounded cerebral or spiritual experience related to the moment of discovering not just the narratives of the art piece, but also the moments when the art works are concretized in the frame of that which is formulaic. It is also the measure in the process of producing art that can articulate the measure of the teleological in the relationship between 'being' and the originary measure of creating art.

Cerebrinity can be that which exhibits the measure with which the representational in the operations of 'signs' is both metaphysical and devoid of the binary measure that defines the traditional structure of 'signs' in the context of modernity. In that a cerebrinous experience induces in the interaction with knowledge the measure of the transcendental in the intellectual space that can be beyond cultural categories, and is comprised of both that which are secular and sacred.

The secular in the sense that it imbues the art-work with historic, social and anthropological connotations that inform the intellect with that which is practical or utilitarian in the context of modernity. Sacred in the sense that it is that space which can induce questions regarding the role of logocentrism as a metaphysical and epistemic facility in the context of modernity that relegates the exigency to the social and cultural periphery.

Logocentrism is the tyranny of the cultural definition manifesting upon the 'sign', it is also 'evidence' of the 'absence' that is originary in the structure of the 'sign'. In that it concretizes 'signs' relationship with the cultural category. Cerebrinity in this context is a consequence of the illumination that is a recognition of the relationship between the 'sign' and the cultural category. It is not an intellectual capacity that seeks to usurp or exert 'being' power over the 'sign' and the cultural category.

The discourse seeks to demonstrate the measure with which an intellectual experience is tantamount to a spiritual experience, when knowledge is an acknowledgment of the illumination that is inherent in the interaction between 'being' and 'signs'. 'Signs' can be characterized as the metaphorical field in which the intellect explores 'meaning' outside of 'being'. Cerebrinity is the measure with which this 'meaning' imbues what is ontological with a measure of indivisibility between 'being' and the 'sign' with connotations to what is didactic and has a relationship to unconscious drives.

Cerebrinity is not about memory, it is rather about being conscious of the measure with which what is didactic about the unconscious becomes embodied into the physical and conscious cerebral drives of 'being'. It is recognition that 'signs' are not comprised of a dualism in their structures but are rather imbued with a measure of synergy that can imbue the cerebral corridors of 'being' with what is illuminating and the ontological location he or she occupies as that which is metaphysical. In this context not only does cerebrinity embody the deconstructionist notion of differance but it also concretizes the measure which exhibits that differance in relation to 'being' attempts to articulate the reconciliation of the structure between physical drives and unconscious drives.

What is illuminating operates and is consistent with the characteristics of the master archetype. This archetype i articulates the relationship between the conscious and the unconscious as characterized by a measure of reconciliation. The discourse of acknowledgements and distinctions states that this reconciliation can be achieved through the facility of the 'sign' and its propensity to relate or establish relationships. Since the notion of cerebrinity presupposes a relationship with the unconscious it is also that which can establish the measure of the 'sign' that has a relationship with the supplement.

The notion of cerebrinity is also that which seeks to demonstrate that a 'sign' cannot be barren of what is supplementary in that this is what enables it to relate or 'appropriate' 'meaning'. In that what is supplementary in the structure of the 'sign' and 'being' enables 'being' to appropriate and conceive of 'self' or 'being' in relation to the supplement. In that to acquire knowledge can be characterized as the means with which 'the real' or reality is supplementing.

The verb form of the word 'supplement' can demonstrate the measure with which first the structure of the 'sign' is imbued with a susceptibility to both acquire and relinquish 'meaning', which also has connotations for the implications of 'presence' and 'absence' in the cerebral or cognitive spaces of 'being'. That being is conscious and cognizant of 'absence' can also characterize illumination or cerebrinity. That it is that space that recognizes that the 'self' is both symbolic and pragmatic, palpable and ephemeral, that even though binaries are crucial in the unfolding and operation of 'being' in order to be imbued with 'meaning' they are contingent on the propensity of 'being' that values order and harmony, chaos and disintegration as the substance of infinite referral.

Cerebrinity is being conscious of the measure in the relationship between 'being' and 'signs' to operate within the structure of 'the real' and exhibits the measure with which the supplementary is already imbued with its own supplementary aspect. Not only is cerebrinity being conscious of the transcendental aspect in the 'sign' but it is also that which exhibits what is formative and didactic in the relationship between 'being' and the supplementary.

This is also the measure with which 'being' becomes conscious of agency or power as an ontological facility, that in the context of modernity becomes pronounced as the primary facility for social, cultural and spiritual orientation. Since 'being' and the symbolic power through the facility of accretion implied in the facility of logocentrism rely on what is conscious, witnessable and informed by positivism. Cerebrinity emphasizes the measure of the pragmatism implied in notions such as thinking, order, harmony in the characteristics of the Apollo archetype.

Not only does this render the relationship between 'being' and knowledge to be imbued with the measure of residual previous experience or the measure of the trace. That according to the discourse of deconstructionism demonstrates that 'signs' are imbued with the 'meanings' of previous epochs or definitions.

The Apollo archetype and cerebrinity both acknowledge this interaction between 'being' and 'signs', in that cerebrinity can also be characterized as the means with which 'being' learns through what is witnessable and positivist. As a measure of appropriating and reconciling conscious and unconscious drives. It is also the means with which 'being' interacts with the 'signs' of language he or she becomes conscious of the fullest measure of representation in the structure of the 'sign' in relation to the community.

The discourse is not stating that 'presence' in the context of cerebrinity is irrelevant, rather on the contrary it concretizes the measure of the didactic in the moment of illumination. This relates it both to the conscious and unconscious through what is witnessable and related to intuition respectively.

This is also the measure with which 'absence' has implications for the 'sign' and the measure in which in the context of 'being' renders what is ontological as that which is metaphysical. In the sense that the ontological is contingent on accretion and the notion of the trace or residual previous experience.

The trace is a notion that can exhibit that what is supplementary and that which is it supplementing are that which can imbue 'being' with his or her own supplementary or supplementing measure. This is also the measure with which his or her 'presence' and 'absence' can become imbued with ontological implications.

If we consider the context of a feral child, where a discourse of 'presence' and 'absence' has implications for cultural formulations. What is cerebrinous necessitates immediate repetition in terms of interacting with 'signs', that this also has implications for the immediacy of the traditional social training, and also has implications for the measure in which the ontological location is characterized by the deconstructionist notion of differance. In that in the context of the feral child 'signs' and their 'meaning' disintegrate but do not the social context. For the feral child interacts with 'signs' in a measure that is characterized by 'new' encounters.

It suffices to state that the measure of mastery is not just that which is related to the creativity or the acquisition of knowledge, but it is also that which has implications for the immediacy of the social and cultural interactions. In that conscious drives are that which operate with the immediacy of the social interaction, but in order to be concretized as formative and didactic they are also that which are imbued with the measure of order and harmony that characterizes mastery of the ontological.

This can be exemplified by an infant who is learning to acquaint him or herself with the physical space, everything is about accumulating or accruing 'signs' and what they mean to the physical and its implications as that which is positivist. That even though the manner in which infants experiment with power is about experimenting with the 'absence' of the 'sign' or facility for this power, in order to master this power it requires repetition but also the necessary security of the 'return' of its 'presence'.

In the context of the art production the experiment is related to the measure of rendering the 'sign' 'barren' of 'meaning', that this strategy demonstrates that the object has a relationship with the supplement and that it also has its supplementary aspect that the facility of the 'being' or agent exhibits. Cerebrinity and its implications for desire also exhibits that the relationship between 'signs' has metaphysical connotations. That they are not just about the negativity that is inherent in the notion of the binary and operates beyond the notion of logocentrism. That experiment with 'absence' in the organic social context has connotations for power in a immediate measure than with future implications.

In the context of producing art cerebrinity is also that which is about perpetual discovering and relinquishing. Form is the means with which the 'new' or creative narratives of the piece become discoursed and necessarily incorporated into the rigidity of the narrative. The object in the context of art production becomes incorporated into its own mythology. Even if this mythology is being repeated, this is also the measure with which 'absence' can be exhibited to be imbued with an aspect of the supplementary. In this context art can be perceived as an institution that is supplementing the object, the mythology itself and the mythology of the subject.

This way the measures of deferral that are inherent in different objects can be perceived they are combined by the facility of the supplement. That art as an institution can be perceived to imbue the measure of the transformational in the object and the manner in which they relate or defer with the propensity to relinquish 'meaning'.

This is significant in the context of cerebrinity in that what is illuminating can 'exhibit' itself to be receptive and complementing to the logic of the supplement. While being capable of illuminating the cultural formulation, and that which is ontological. In the context of art this is the measure with which a cerebrinous intellectual experience can demonstrate that deferral is necessitated by the originary breach of communication. This is not just between 'being' and objects, but the 'meaning' that can be generated and accrued between objects.

Cerebrinity seeks to demonstrate that the breach has ontological implications in the context of art production not only as a measure of the transformational and the supplementary. It also as the measure that demonstrates that agency is an originary facility related to 'being' and his relationship with the unconscious. If we compare the unconscious to a forest for example, the perpetual flux that a forest is characterized with makes it an ideal metaphor for the flux and perpetual nature of the mind and its propensity to incorporate and appropriate 'new' knowledge and 'signs'.

Art exposes the breach as that which is based on communication and the immediacy that characterizes the social context, It also exposes the measure in which the immediacy in the social transaction is deemed to deprive 'being' of agency or power. That the breach is inculcated to not be 'present', rather what is deemed 'present' is the 'absence' of the traditional social training or the relevant 'initio'. The teleological relevance of art is not to state that the breach does not have cultural or ontological relevance. Rather the intellectual and spiritual clarity that is implicated in the notion of cerebrinity can demonstrate that the breach is consciousness and agency that has connotations for the notion of a master.

Jung has exhibited that the notion of the master does not only have implications for intellectual prowess, but it also has implications for psychological development and comprehension of social navigation. Cerebrinity is being conscious of the fact that what is formative and didactic has implications for enlightenment. That the breach also has implication for enlightenment as much as it has implications for knowledge, even though it is independent of 'being' it is crucial for establishing a relationship with the 'signs' and the unconscious.

In the context of modernity this notion of 'absence' in the structure of the relationship between 'being' and knowledge has implications. This 'absence' is imbued with connotations of power and lack of power, it is also the location where what is metaphysical about this 'absence' is related to the notion of logocentrism. Also in the context of modernity if this 'absence' is imbued with a measure of the metaphysical with existential connotations, then it can be demonstrated that the originary agency in 'being' in the production of art is the originary agency in 'being' consistent and similar to archaic man.

In that if the unconscious is the repository for 'signs' and art is the arena upon which these 'signs' find a field upon, not just to discover 'meaning' but to also manifest the measure with which repetition is the bases for accretion and the epistemic. Art is also a facility that validates knowledge and the accretion that has been accrued through the facility of creativity and the narratives that artists imbue 'signs' with.

The notion of cerebrinity is related to art to the extent that it concretizes that which is spiritual about interacting with knowledge. In
the context of modernity where the measure of 'absence' of the
traditional social training is imbued with a measure of teleological
and ontological connotations. The intellectual space then has become a space of contestation in that 'being' has been reduced to the
myths and narratives of his or her originary culture. That they are
oppositional or combative towards the symbolic power which characterizes sovereignty in the cultural dispensation.

To the extent that notions of power in this context are that which
are not related to this measure of 'absence' in modernity, unlike in
the   context   of   the originary culture,   where   the   'absence'
represented possibility or what is spiritual about the encounter with
knowledge. Not as that which is beyond the ontological clutches of
'being', but as that which can be related to the unconscious through
the facility of intuition and what is originary about it.

In the context of art, this is the measure with which the ontological is 'barren' of agency or the necessary 'initio'. It becomes necessary for the 'being' to inculcate that which is originary in relation to
a didactic relationship with the symbolic power. He or she also has
to 'invent' existential narratives in relation to the symbolic power. Theses can be personal, historical, cultural or political, what
makes art production that which can be characterized as cerebrinous is that it can reconcile the measure which is illuminating
and ontological about this 'absence'. That is also that which illumi-
nates this 'absence' as that which 'being' has to be conscious of in
order to compensate for.

Even though cerebrinity can be induced by this breach it is also
that which through the facility of art exhibit that 'being' is the medium that exhibits that this 'absence' is part of the cultural dispensation. That it is symbolic to the negative character or the 'nature'
of sovereignty that characterizes the cultural dispensation.

The notion of cerebrinity seeks to demonstrate that the breach is
auto-referential to the extent that since 'being' is barren of the traditional social training. He or she has to be conscious of the measure which imbues 'signs' with the facility for deferral as that which
is not characterized by a binary. That being conscious of this
is originary and imbues the relationship between 'being' and the
'sign' with what is originary and supplementary. That it supplements the notion of logocentrism as both that which is epistemic

and related to the symbolic power which is also relates 'being' to the unconscious.

The notion of cerebrinity is an intellectual manifestation for the measure in which the 'sign' has an originary relationship with the 'being'. The discourse of acknowledgements and distinction seeks to demonstrate that 'being' can also be characterized by an 'absence' in his or her initial encounter with the 'sign'. This 'absence' is evidence in the desire for that which is didactic, through the process of referral that enables a propensity for the 'sign' to relinquish and accrue.

Cerebrinity as a facility for immediate intellectual postulation and examination, is similar in structure to the lack of a binary opposition between being and 'sign'. This is according to the didactic implication in the context of modernity and the symbolic power. The symbolic power postulates that 'being' does not have an originary relationship with 'signs' in a confrontational or combative manner. Rather this relationship through a desire for the didactic emphasizes accretion and relinquishing. The 'absence' that is inherent in 'being' also justifies the notion of the supplement being related to the collective unconscious as both a facility for accretion and a didactic facility. In the case of a feral experience for example, the 'being' with his or her implications for 'absence' that is organic, becomes contingent on the organic propensities for psychological reconciliation. In that in the context of a feral experience when the 'being' encounters a modern context for example, his or her organic fragmented experience becomes apparent. The social and cultural disorientation necessitates a relationship with 'signs' that in the context of the encounter can be characterized as spiritual or illuminating. This can also be pronounced in the feral person learning about God or some other spiritual experiences that also operate as didactic facilities.

The discourse of acknowledgments and distinctions seeks to demonstrate that art movements like Dadaism, provide this sense of illuminations in the community or individual's relationship with knowledge and 'signs', a collective cerebrinity unfolded and characterized the cultural dispensation in the context of modernity. What ensued was a negation of the processes of accretion in the 'signs' that are imbued with universal didactic connotations, for example instead of emphasizing universal brotherly love people where conscripted for war, instead of the symbolic power being cognizant of the community's needs it imposed violence and propagated values with sinister connotations where being harbored by communities other than the one's they lead or rule.

A cerebrinous experience can be possible in a context of great transformation, where an organic 'absence' ensues in the cultural dispensation, where it is operational between the notion of the supplement and the accretion that has already informed 'signs' in the cultural dispensation. 'Signs' in a context of a cultural breakdown, their relationship to the supplement becomes pronounced as a referral didactic facility. They also demonstrate that the notion of 'absence' is always already operation in the structure of 'signs'. In times of political crises the 'sign' can be detected to have an overt secondary or aiding operation. It becomes pronounced as this 'supplementary' didactic facility that enables the collective unconscious and universal didactic notions to be informed by this structure of 'absence' and accretion.

Art practice is able to discern the location of the supplement in context of social upheaval, in that art practice is cognizant that it also 'emanates' from the recesses of the supplement through its propensity for accretion and relinquishing. Since in the context of social upheaval there is an overt sense of relinquishing of meaning or 'absence' in the structure of 'signs', the symbolic power as an image for social didactic structure becomes questioned. Its relationship to the supplement can also be questioned. In turn they symbolic power can posit questions about its relationship to the supplementary as a means for universal didactic implications. That as an image it can 'breakdown' is also a cerebrinous realization, that it can be restored demonstrates the propensity of the supplement to operate as a fullest measure of presence, and the symbolic power to have desire for what Deconstructionism describes as an image of "plenitude" (Reynolds, J, (http:// www.iep.utm.edu/derrida).

Gale states that "those subsequently grouped around the banner of Dadaism....took an ideological stand. They did not simply hold up a mirror to society: they demanded attention. They exposed its moral decay with ferocity and wit unprecedented for the arts" (Dada and Surrealism, 5).

Cerebrinity can demonstrate that this was achieved through the strategy of abstraction in the execution and practice of art. Abstraction became a mechanism with which 'signs' assumed 'independence' or 'absence'. This 'independence' with its overt operational implications marked the manner in which its previous inter-dependence was not rigid and austere as 'traditional' thought purported but oscillates between accretion and relinquishing of 'meaning'. This was exemplified in Dada through abstraction of 'signs' both as physical and non-physical elements. The 'sign' did not relinquish its previous meaning, Dadaist strategy made overt its cultural or traditional trappings. Dadaist strategy also made overt that the image of the symbol can breakdown from within itself, abstraction was able to render 'signs' a facility for reconciling with the mechanism that provides them with 'meaning' and accretion. When the image of the symbolic power disintegrates, its operation as a 'mirror' for the didactic facility becomes overt, in this process of the disintegration its fragmentary nature becomes overt. This is the location where its operation as an image of a universal plenitude becomes questioned, whether it's a plenitude at all "where it is assigned in the structure by a mark of emptiness" (Reynolds, J) citing (O.G 144).

Cerebrinity is not only intellectual spiritual illumination, but it is also the organic inclination to demonstrate that the 'emptiness' or 'absence' is already always operational. That when the structure of the supplement is questioned it is not redundant rather it demonstrates the notion of the supplementary requires a facility for reconciliation. In that the symbolic power becomes demonstrated as a supplementary mechanism, rather than pronouncing the 'absent' supplement. It therefore in the context of social upheaval as Dadaism demonstrated requires a reconciliation facility. The 'absence' of the supplement renders the image of plenitude that the symbolic power is inculcated to characterize as that which is fragmented in relation to the supplement. What is supplementary can be characterized to be the national paraphernalia that is representational and contained in the malleability of policy making and devising law. Their terms of interacting between spiritual institutions and the reconciliation of accrued or historic events. So that it characterizes in the intellectual space a presence. Since this presence has a role of realizing the orginary didactic desire in the structure of the symbolic power. What is 'absent' then can operate as the means with which it is an aid to the structure of plenitude. Where it necessitates the presence of the supplementary or that it can be evidenced. The symbolic power through the reconciliatory function of art movements like Dadaism, can be demonstrated to be characterized by a desire for the didactic by enabling or structuring a relationship with the supplement. In the context of the symbolic power, where it diffuses its supplementary operations, the necessary substitution between the 'absence' for the didactic through the supplementary becomes overt in the context of collective social upheaval. What is revolutionary about art movements like Dadaism is that through this 'absence' what ensues during a social upheaval is that they provide a reconciliation facility between the symbolic power and the supplement. They also provide the means with which the community can instigate their own agency in relation to the supplementary. The supplement can be detected to be a repository for auto-illumination, for the transformation propensity of 'signs', for the realization for an originary relationship with the community, and an intellectual space for the abstract or 'abstract' operation of supplementary concepts.

Chapter 3

Art, Referral and the Supplementary/Supplement

In the context of modernity the structure of 'signs' does not have connotations for deferral, as critical theory has established. The discourse had to define and explicate the terms and conditions upon which this structure in 'signs' is reified.

It did this by relating the community to its own relationship with 'signs', that it has an originary or organic relationship with the supplement. That the notion of hysteridence through this originary deferral propensity on the part of the community also demonstrates the measure with which 'being' and the community are organically imbued with their own agency.

The chapter will also demonstrate that the structure with which the symbolic power operates in the context of modernity, is consistent with the structure of the maternal or germination aspect. That notions like cerebrinity and hysteridence are manifestations on the part of the community to 'return' to the maternal figure in the context of modernity. This is concretized in the context of modernity, by relating to the logic of the logocentrism in terms of deferring towards the supplement.

The chapter has sought to demonstrate the substance of relating to the originary is characterized by 'being' establishing a relationship with it. Art is a facility in the context of modernity with which this relationship can be established.

The chapter also seeks to demonstrate that hysteridence is a socially organic formative tool that instigates discourse of the fullest measure of presence, through art movements like Dadaism, by interrogating the value of material ethics.

This it seeks to demonstrate has implications for the structures of signification in the dispensation being characterized by an 'absence' on both the context of the community and the context of the symbolic power.

That the essentialism that has been demonstrated by discourse of deconstructionism in the structures of the 'signs', the work seeks to demonstrate that through art, the structure of the 'signifier' interrogates the structure of the 'sign'.

It also seeks to exhibit that the dual operation of the 'sign' in the context of art the 'absent' structure of the symbolic power has a reconciliation relationship with the supplement.

By incorporating or considering Kristeva's notion of the phallic symbolic, and the image of desiring a return to the maternal image that characterizes the structure of the relationship between the community and the symbolic power. The discourse wants to demonstrate the measure with which the structure of 'signs' in the context of the community has to demonstrate a desire in relating to the symbolic power.

Of discourse in the structure of the supplement

The discourse of acknowledgement and distinctions seeks to demonstrate that the facility of the supplement has its own representational and auto-referential aspect which concretizes the notion of the initium, both in relation to 'itself' and in relation to the 'presence' that can inform a particular context. This is significant in that the notion of referral induces auto-recognition of 'self' and the didactic facilities that 'self' has at his or her disposal. In the context of the supplement referral applies in the same measure in that, 'presence' operates in the symbolic sense with which 'being' auto-affection operates, both in the measure of 'desire' for referral and in the sense of the passivity that informs the auto-symbolism of the supplement in relation to the relationships that can be established.

The supplement cannot conceive of 'itself' but it is imbued with a facility of auto-referential, and that this is the measure with which the 'sign' and the cultural formulation are capable of establishing a symbolic relationship with the supplement. In this manner that which is related to the 'absence' that the supplement also symbolizes is related to desire or referral for 'being' and the 'sign', and the measure with which this desire instigates conceptions of the fullest measure of presence.

In the context of art the fullest measure of presence occupies this symbolic location of 'presence' and 'absence', which is crucial to the mercurial operation of the 'sign' being able to relinquish and acquire 'meaning'. Mercurial in the sense that in the structure of the supplement there is also the measure of auto-referential and the referral that the cultural formulation can incite. What is crucial in the context of art production is the measure which can exhibit that what is symbolic about auto-affection also has a referral relationship with the supplement. Like 'being', art production is able to incite conceptions of the fullest measure of presence.

Modernity has inculcated that referral in the structure of the 'sign' can induce the measure of what is oppositional to the symbolic power and that it is imbued with teleological implications in relation to the supplement. This is reflected in the logic of the logocentrism, as not only a symbolic facility for the desire for what is didactic in relation to the supplement, it is also the measure that exhibits in the context of modernity that the 'sign' has been imbued and cultivated with overt existential connotations. That the didactic is imbued with existential connotations in order to exhibit in the cultural dispensation that the fullest measure of presence and the manner in which 'being' relates to knowledge should be related in a metaphoric measure in relation to the symbolic power.

The existential logic and its isolationist measure can be inculcated in relation to the fullest measure of presence through the facility of collective unconscious. This in order to justify the teleological relevance of the immediacy of the social contract and the traditional social training. The teleological relevance of the supplement cannot be refuted through this strategy, but it is also that which cannot be reduced to a measure of the representational that has relevance to the isolated and binary notion of 'origins' after the advent of the substitution.

This notion of the isolated individuality in the context of modernity only justifies the logic of the traditional social training, and isolates the originary notion of what is didactic from the context prior the substitution. Art practice in the context of modernity discourses this measure of the existential in relation to the symbolic power. It has been imbued with reactionary and anarchist connotations outside the notion of economics, through the logic that these ethics or values are barren or not informed by logocentrism. Not only does this pronounce the isolation of the individual, it also renders the relationship between the symbolic power and the supplement, susceptible to the role of agency that 'being' occupies.

Art practice as an institution also pronounces the measure with which what is metaphysical in the operation of the 'sign' concretizes the measure of agency in 'being' and his didactic relationship to the supplement. That the measure with which art induces a cerebrinous intellectual experience pronounces the didactic as that which also has connotations for the metaphysical.

Not only does this imbue the measure of the existential in the context of modernity with auto-referential auto-affection, it also imbues it with a relationship with the collective unconscious that what is 'independent' in the symbolic power renders 'being' a metaphysical entity, but also imbued with the propensity to refer.

The measure of the 'sign' to refer the deconstruction project has demonstrated is contingent on the supplement through comprehending the metaphysical element in the 'sign'. Where the ambiguity of 'presence' subsumes the measure of 'absence', that not only relates it to the binary of physical absence, but also the 'absence' of 'meaning' or metaphysical meaning. The discourse is not stating that 'being' is a conduit or some agent of metaphysical interaction between the object and the intellectual in some mystical sense, rather art production in both archaic man and in modern man, the object instigates what is mystical about the supplement and that this is the measure with which the 'sign' and the object refer.

That 'being' is also contingent on referral, that his or her relationship with the supplement exhibits that auto-affection is a measure which differentiates the 'absence' from the 'presence' of both desire and referral of that desire. In the context of art practice in the modern context, referral of desire to the supplement is still related to what is didactic otherwise it would not discourse the fullest measure of presence through which the 'sign' and its referral propensities can justify its 'presence' or its presence.

The notion of cerebrinity pronounces the metaphysical measure of the 'sign' and its referral propensities in that for 'being', in order to imbue auto-affection with ontological connotations that relate to the epistemic, the measure of the trace or infinite referral in the 'sign' has to be acknowledged. In the context of art practice this measure of the 'sign' to be imbued with the metaphysical, is also the measure with which what is epistemic refers in the cultural dispensation to the extent that it can maintain what is didactic, as that which is metaphysical and related to the unconscious.

In the context of archaic man, the initial stages of referral to the supplement where characterized by a measure of the ambiguity of referral, where the 'sign' acknowledged its passive location as its referral facility. This passivity was characterized by the necessity of differentiating between what is didactic about desire that the 'absence' of the 'sign' and the desire for the presence or 'presence' of what was witnessable precipitated in the form of that which can be reconciled in the creative expression or 'sign'. Not only were these manifestations a measure with which the supplement is a referral facility, they were also indicative of the metaphysical element in referral, where and when the function of the 'sign' was reinforced by the originary 'absence' that induced desire for the didactic.

Art practice and referral are desire manifesting in the ontological context of 'being', they are also the measure that exhibits the measure with which 'being' is independent from the 'sign' in relation to the cultural production. This is significant in the context of modernity in that 'being' is an entity that is contingent on relating to power and has to be cognizant of relinquishing this power. Where as archaic man and his relationship to his agency or propensity for referral since, it was appropriation that was emphasized, the metonymic or displacement was that which was imbued with the metaphysical as a didactic capacity for orientation. Not only did this enable 'being' to operate in a measure that inform accretion, but it also induced what is metaphysical in the location or cerebral operations of 'being'.

In the modern context of art practice it is the 'sign' or object that has primary metaphysical connotations, in that these connotations are imbued with a measure of referral and non-referral or relinquishing is testament to the extent of accretion, and the measure of 'signs' in the unconscious having its own energy or structure. As Kristeva states that 'being' can be in control of 'signs' even if he or she is not conscious of them, this in the context of art production this can be exemplified by the necessity to transform the 'meaning' of a 'sign' or that which is metaphoric about it in order to pronounce or illuminate discourse. The notion of 'being' being able to 'control' 'signs' in the unconscious stems from the measure in 'being' to desire what is didactic and imbue it with universal connotations or that it is always already imbued with universal connotations. This is exemplified in Oliver who states that "for Kristeva, Other is a space of metaphorical shifting in which symbols are substituted for, or condensed with, drive force"

That this also concretizes the measure of the 'sign' as a supplementary tool, that 'being' is also a supplementary tool with a propensity to concretize the referral propensity of the 'sign'. What is cerebrinous is this propensity to be conscious of the 'sign' in its operations to relinquish 'meaning' even in the unconscious, that this is what enables the transformational aspect in the 'sign' to be related to accretion.

Art practice in its teleological manifestation pronounces the measure of 'absence' or the differentiation of between 'absence' and 'presence' in the 'sign'. That the propensity for transformation is informed by an 'otherness' within the structure of the 'sign', that modernity has cultivated into the cultural dispensation. Art production 'interprets' the 'sign' in a measure that is related to the transformational element in the structure of the 'sign.'

In that how it has accrued seeks to demonstrate that the metaphoric operates as a 'signifier', but the 'signifier' in the plethora of accretion has been imbued with 'other' elements which have enabled appropriation and relinquishing. The artist as a conduit for social commentary utilizes this facility as not that which is reactionary or informed by conflict but as that which seeks to exhibit that accretion is related to the supplement. That what is teleological about the operation of the 'sign' in the context of art is the propensity for 'free association' that also informs accretion and relinquishing. In the context of art, the teleological goal is not 'othering' in the sense of concretizing a binary, rather to 'other' is to exhibit the ablative propensity for production of the piece with its relationship with the symbolic power. Hence the 'sign' operating within the social and culturally accrued paradigm that has been informed by the accretion in the facility of the initium or the enunciative field in the cultural dispensation.

Parallel to this is how the unconscious operates in the same measure, in that art production demonstrates that 'being' can be in controlled of 'signs' in location of the conscious, where their metaphorical measure is didactic and accrued. That this is the location where what is supplementary about the 'sign' becomes apparent, it is also the location in which the independence of the 'sign' and the existential measure in 'being' becomes delineated.

In the context of art practice this delineation takes place at a didactic and symbolic level, that the 'sign' is not only a facility for referral, it also instigates discourse and concretizes what is teleological about accretion. In that in the social context, the symbolic is utilized to exhibit that difference is an orientation facility is imbued with contemporary definition of the 'sign'. Art also demonstrates that the 'sign' is a 'signifier' when it is invoked in the context, that the 'signifier' then becomes the instigator of discourse but not its

measure. For art it becomes significant to establish difference between the 'source' of a discourse or that which instigates the 'signifier' in a context and the intention of the 'signifier' in a context.
This way the measure of the metonymic or transformational in the
'sign' can be detected for its contemporary symbolic utilization and
for the artistic goals of the art piece.

In art categories of 'signs' are significant to the extent that
they concretize discourse, they also concretize that a 'sign' is not
comprised of a measure of essentialism, this way 'signs' can be
detected for their symbolic and didactic function. It cannot be refuted that art is always already in a binary communication with the
symbolic power, therefore the analytical element that art production and art practice instigates discourses the subjectivity that characterize a relationship with the supplement. That through being
conscious of the supplementary operation of the 'sign' through the
accretion and relinquishing of its ambiguous structure, art is able to
discourse the extent to which the facility of logocentrism can maintain its essentialism.

Art can exhibit that logocentrism can impose an internal subordination within the structure of this 'sign', the 'independence' of the
supplement is symbolic to the extent that referral cannot be instigated by the supplement itself. Rather it is instigated by presence or
'presence', that 'being' can refer to the 'absence' that is symbolic in
the context of the supplement. This way it can never impose or
'dictate' 'meaning', rather meaning becomes embroiled in measure
of reciprocity between the 'sign' and the supplement. In the context of logocentrism, there is a specific context which is identified to
be the source of the notion, if there is a source for a didactic facility,
then this facility can be characterized by a trace, where referral and
relinquishing concretize its didactic structure.

In the context of modernity, that which is imbued with a structure
of the didactic has to be cognizant of logocentrism, it also has to be
cognizant of the metaphysical aspect in logocentrism that
was concretized by the context of the substitution. Since the substitution was deemed barren of metaphysical connotations, it incorporated the metaphysical within the utilitarian structure of the
'sign', by emphasizing the positivist and witnessable as primary
orientation facilities in the operation of the 'sign'. Since positivism
is a notion that subsumes what is ontological and existential as
palpable orientation facilities, the measure with which 'being' is
contingent on the didactic measure of the symbolic power, has

inculcated that 'being' is to some extent not in control of 'signs' even the 'signs' that he or she is conscious of. Art practice does not refute the didactic relevance of the symbolic power, rather it discourses its engagement with the originary. That the symbolic power has instigated a relationship with the spiritual institution as separate from the methodological implications of symbolic or institutional theory, or as that which is primarily metaphysical.

The deconstructionist project has demonstrated that the binary structure that resulted from the logic of separating the spiritual institution from the symbolic power and its bureaucratic structures has inculcated that what is positivist and metaphysical occupy separate locations in the cerebral spaces of 'being'. Since there is a measure of 'absence' in the context of modernity, 'signs' are that which operate primarily in a condensation measure, this way the symbolic power is able to exhibit that orientation facilities are that which can exhibit that the fullest measure of presence must accommodate diversity but also that the context of the substitution was imbued with a binary structure. The binary structure was that which exhibited in the new cultural paradigm that 'being' is the measure with which the condensation facility was related to the collective unconscious. This way the logic of diversity could be related to an orientation sensibility that was informed by a pure and essentialist structure, that also this way what is didactic was that which could discourse notions of origins and the originary in relation to communities that are diverse or multi-cultural.

That the spiritual institution in the context of modernity is inculcated as a subordinate facility, whose didactic operation is limited, in that the deconstructionist project has exhibited that it occupies the location of 'absence', in the structure of the 'sign'. The facility of logocentrism is contingent on the 'presence' of 'signs'. That this is exemplified by the measure with which 'being', relies on the positivist as an orientation facility that the spiritual institution can imbue with metaphysical connotations and implications. The subordination facility in the structure of a 'sign' enables the 'being' to imbue it with displacement propensities, in that this is the measure in the context of art production that takes advantage of the 'absence' that is connoted by the subordinate facility in the structure of the 'sign'.

Art production concretizes the displacement facility of the 'sign' in the unconscious and the conscious in a measure that is not about power, but that is about the agency that is connoted in the condensation operation of the 'sign' in the context of the substitution. Art also concretizes the condensation facility of the 'sign' through its teleological relevance or its relationship to the transformational propensities of referral in relation to the supplement, that this is also the measure with which 'being' concretizes his or her agency.

That what is supplementary in the operation of the 'sign' exhibits that accretion and the epistemic are didactic to the extent that even though what necessitates them in the context of modernity is the measure of 'absence'. This is how the 'presence' of the didactic facilities of the symbolic power are contingent on the agency of 'being'. No more is this more pronounced in the context of art production, in the measure with which 'being' becomes imbued with originary referral propensities, in both the condensation and displacement facilities respectively.

With the discourse of acknowledgements and distinctions the 'sign' is imbued with a malleability that enables it to refer while being cognizant of accretion and the propensity to relinquish. In the context of art practice the didactic connotations of the 'sign' become imbued with transformational connotations. These connotations operate with both metonymic and metaphoric implications. This way the multi dimensionality of a context can be detected and inculcated within the discourse the 'sign' or the artwork seeks to engage. This is also the arena within which abstraction assumes a structure, where discourse and accretion operate in tandem. The 'meaning' of the 'sign' and discourse are simultaneously present and 'absent', it is an ambiguity that demonstrates the 'sign' and the discourse's contingency on the supplement. The image of the maternal is significant to the extent that it postulates that this 'absence' is 'present' and is operational, operational through its germination and propensity for accretion. It also suggests accumulation in both the contemporary and historic contexts, where the 'sign' can be exhibited to be imbued with immediacy. Referral in the maternal image also implies the exhaustion in the social context that modernity purports structures the operation of didactic implications and 'signs'.

In the context of social upheaval as in the one that Dadaism the art movement emerged in, necessitated the individual 'being' to separate from the maternal implication of protection and care that the symbolic power is organically imbued with. The 'sign' with it being already always imbued with the propensity to relinquish 'meaning', also has to master this separation from the maternal image in the structures of the symbolic power.

This way the 'emptiness' that characterizes the symbolic power, in a context of social upheaval it can be detected to be alien from the community. This way it cannot only detected in the violent or negative manner in which it disseminates formative or didactic strategies, it can also be detected in the manner in which it relies on the collective body of the community to re-establish itself.

What Dadaism was able to do, was to help the community discern the intrinsic operation of a 'sign'. In the sense that, if the symbolic power is able to relinquish its relationship with a 'sign' then the notion of the supplement as an organic aid to the 'sign' can be detected to be imbued with maternal and gestation implications. The community is then left to their own devises to devise their own symbolic order that is organic to the social context. That to an extent challenges the notion and strategy of an exhaustible operation of a 'sign'. When the community devises its own symbolic order within the context of advanced modernity, that image or 'fantasy of the phallic mother'(http://english.fju.edu.tw/lctd/asp/theory/theory_works/69/study.ht) becomes concretized as a conception of a didactic desire, where and when the subjective propensity of a symbolic power is no longer able to fulfill its role. This substitution is also that which not only instigates discourse around the 'presence' of the supplement, it also instigates discourse around the originary desire for the didactic to be imbued with a pleasure principle. This pleasure principle can be related to subjectivity and operation of the maternal image in both its germination processes but also when manifestation transpires, beyond germination and into the arena of 'meaning'.

In the context of the emergence of Dadaism the pleasure principle manifested in the communal solidarity that characterized the activism and production of art. The significant role of formula or theory in the art movement concretized the subjective operation of the movement. This way it could be detected to be a mechanism for substitution for the maternal or germination operation that is necessary when the community is contingent on the originary relationship of the supplement. Since the 'absence' that ensues when the symbolic power relinquishes its relationship to 'signs', the pleasure principle ensues when the community is able to devise its symbolic order from the facility of the 'empty' supplement. By devising its own symbolic order the community is able to conceive its existence in relation to itself instead of the void that the symbolic power instigates in a context of social and political upheaval.

The symbolic order from the maternal image that the community devises does not instigate a combative relationship with the notion of the 'phallic mother'. Since the risk of losing an identity is already 'present' in a context of a social upheaval, then the 'new' symbolic order concretizes the measure with which identity is already always contingent on the community being cognizant of the secondary operation of the supplement being imbued with referral mechanism that is independent from the symbolic power.

Herein lies the notion that returning to the maternal is imbued with a pleasure principle, in that manifestation has to transpire through the 'new' symbolic order the community devises. This discourse seeks to demonstrate that this pleasurable return to the maternal figure is tantamount to Hermes' return to his mother after he stole his brother the God Apollo's cattle (http://www.myastrologybook.com/Mercury-Hermes-Trismegistus-Thoth.htm,
Carl Woebcke). The image of protection and care this mythological narrative exhibits is indicative first of the necessity to separate from the maternal in the sense that Hermes is said to be in his infancy upon embarking on the adventure. When metaphorically related to context of advanced capitalism or the context in which Dadaism emerged, it can be detected that not only does a return to the maternal figure entail a pleasure principle but it also through the organic relationship with 'signs' help induce creativity, both collective and individual.

Art practice then demonstrates that the supplement or the secondary element in the structuring of didactic principles requires a reconciliation facility. That pronounces the maternal figure, not just as arbitrary but that it is structured through the subjectivity of cultural formulations and the subjectivity of the symbolic power in the context of modernity. In the immediacy that characterizes art practice and art production the necessity of this reconciliation has intellectual and spiritual connotations related to the measure with which the individual is imbued with a cultural definition if he or she has the facility to relinquish.

The structure of the symbolic order that the community devises operates as the measure with which the intellectual substance of the 'new' order legitimizes the supplement. This way it concretizes itself in an auto-referential manner as that which justifies its operation as supplementary. In that the 'new' symbolic order in a context ravaged by social upheaval must also auto-reference like the symbolic power, this way the order that is purported can be detected to have moral connotations that relate to the secondary operation of the supplement.

Dadaism or art movements achieve this by demonstrating that there is an organic unity within the community that symbolic power in the context of advanced modernity does not account for. That this is related to the measure with which 'signs' in the social context auto-reference and cannot be exhausted in their operation but are perpetuated by the originary breach of communication where what is repeated has implications for self-presence and what cannot be conveyed has connotations for the didactic or formative.

Chapter 4

The Epistemic as Metaphoric
and Metonymic

In this chapter the discourse seeks to demonstrate the measure with which the epistemic is imbued with an 'absent' structure in the context of the community. The discourse has to demonstrate the measure with which the 'absence' in the context of the community being imbued with an 'absent' structure.

The work also seeks to demonstrate the measure with which art practice can demonstrate how 'being' desires a relationship with the symbolic power. By exhibiting the significance of the ontological in relating to the symbolic power, that the 'absent' structure that informs the location of the community in its relationship with the symbolic power is contingent on 'being' desire for the didactic.

Through art practice, the 'absence' that characterizes the location of the community will be demonstrated becomes reified in the accretion that takes place within the structure of the epistemic.

The discourse seeks to demonstrate how the symbolic power has at its disposal the propensity to demonstrate that 'signs' require a containing principle that this facility operates through the devolution of power the symbolic power has at its disposal. The discourse will seek to demonstrate how the 'being' is characteristically imbued with the dual capacity to implicate towards the symbolic power and be conscious of his capacity to produce in the context of the artist and be cognizant of the nature of implicating towards the symbolic power.

This chapter also seeks to demonstrate the measure with which art operates primarily with metonymic connotations. It will seek to exhibit the measure with which as the deconstructionist oeuvre has sought to demonstrate, that in the logic of exhaustion in the immediate social context, it becomes impossible to desire in person or through 'presence', where the 'being' in his 'absence' of didactic implication towards the symbolic power being characterized by an 'absence'. How 'being' in the social context relates to 'signs' through deferral.

That in the context of art 'signs' operate with overt metonymic implications that can demonstrate the measure with which if 'being' is in constant adequation with one self, he or she relates to 'signs' through deferral or imbuing transformational connotations to the 'sign'.

That this form of metaphysical relinquishing can constitute the pleasure principle and manifests as creativity, agency, power and facility to juxtapose contexts and 'signs'.

Of the metonymic episteme

The epistemic subsumes knowledge, learning, creativity, and deferral. In the context of modernity art movements have been necessitated by the dichotomy structure in the relationship between the symbolic power and the community. In that they have interrogated the measure of subordination and submission in the structure of the 'sign' related to the location of the community in this dichotomy. To interrogate and discourse the structure of a 'sign' is not only a manifestation of the originary jurisdiction or agency in 'being'. It is also to interrogate the measure with which what is didactic and accrued in the context of the symbolic power has relevance for the logocentric.

This is also the means with which what is didactic in the context of modernity imbues the structure of the social transaction with a measure of immediacy in order to demonstrate that logocentrism in a diverse context caters for the dominant location in the dichotomy. That the metaphysical operation of art in the social context is consistent with the metaphysical 'presence' of logocentrism, and that the measure of self-implication to the symbolic power is imbued with the same structure as the originary and metaphysical connotations. They are both informed by a measure of transience that can demonstrate that 'being' and the referral structure of the logocentrism have implications for a relationship with the supplement.

The art movement supplements both the supplement and 'itself', this way its discourse becomes imbued with a measure of the ontological that subsumes agency as an originary facility with implications for being interrogated by the didactic logic of the symbolic power. Art movements operate with the logic of the 'sign' from an epistemic perspective in order to concretize their accretion in the context of modernity and in the context of 'being' to concretize the logic of 'signs' operating in the conscious and unconscious. Not only does this subsume what is didactic, it also engages the discourse of 'absence' and 'presence' that informs the logic behind cultural or social training.

Inherent in the notion of logocentrism is the measure to defer 'meaning', but there is also the measure to supplement. This supplementary operation does not cater for fullest measure of presence in a cultural dispensation. Rather it operates a condensation facility in relation to the cultural formulation.

In the context of the substitution from the rural to the urban context, the measure of deferral that is inherent in the structure of the logocentrism became imbued with specialization connotations in relation to disseminating the 'new' didactic and in relation to 'being', and the essentialist or 'pure' operation of a 'sign'. This resulted in the measure of art discoursing the propensity in the cultural training to enable the 'sign' to 'stop' deferral, that it can be safely stated that the 'sign' has been inculcated to have accrued enough 'meaning' in order to operate as a condensation facility. Where if referral has ceased, it would be a 'sign' whose didactic implication 'being' is conscious of as 'new' or unable to 'control' in relation to the operation of how 'signs' accrue in the unconscious.

The deconstructionist project has exhibited that a 'sign' in order to operate with metaphoric implications or operate as a condensation facility, in order to be imbued with epistemic connotations, 'being' and the symbolic power, with the facilities for dissemination, all have to be cognizant of the accretion. Both their supplementary or symbolic operations have connotations for the 'absence' that is crucial in the operation of a 'sign' in the context of modernity and the symbolic power. 'Absence' in the context of the epistemic exhibits that deferral and 'signs' are that which are supplemented by the supplement. That if the community is to be conscious of an 'absence' in the structure of the 'sign', there has to have been a measure of accretion that is related to desire for what is didactic related to the operation of a 'sign'. This can be detected in contexts when what is didactic about a 'sign' has been relinquished or rendered passive or submissive.

The metaphoric operation of the 'sign' can also be exhibited to be influenced and crucial to the notion of accretion. In that not only can it demonstrate an epistemic operation, it also exhibits and concretizes a relationship with the supplement. Art practice can exhibit this facility in the 'sign' as a facility for infinite referral but also for a measure that what is ambiguous in the operation of a 'sign' incorporates both condensation and displacement propensities. The discourse of acknowledgements and distinctions is not stating that in order to be concrete a 'sign' assumes this facility simultaneously or in the same context, but that art exhibits that displacement cannot be imbued with 'meaning' if it is not imbued with referral from the condensation operation.

The displacement operation becomes stagnant in the finished artifact, but in order to be conceived and disseminated as didactic or as a 'moral' tool. It has to include the epistemic as that which instigates what is transformational in both the cerebral space or unconscious, but also in the social context. Art artifact becomes imbued with transformational propensity while being cognizant of the condensation facility being imbued with accrued 'meaning'. This way as a displacement facility it can be demonstrated to be both didactic and a facility for didactic instruction. So that the artifact operates within the cultural paradigm or the framework of accretion that is informed by logocentrism, that modernity has made the foundations of the structure of referral in the cultural dispensation.

Art values and pronounces the role of the 'presence' of a 'sign', both in the physical and in the abstract cerebral spaces of 'being'. That this is the measure with which art exhibits itself to be supplementary and not just transformational. It also how it exhibits to be imbued with a measure of the symbolic that automatically includes both the condensation and the displacement facilities in the structure of the 'sign'. Not only does this exhibit the supplementary and transformational function, it also exhibits the measure with which 'absence' in the 'sign' can be symbolic, in both the cerebral spaces and when this 'absence' is referred in relation to physical implications. That art appreciation or non-appreciation is also defined by the impossibility of desiring the art object in 'person', that there has to a measure of 'absence' in the conscious spaces of 'being'.

In the context of art, it is impossible to desire 'presence' 'in person', but through being cognizant of the transformational manifestation of the art object, but also through the 'presence' of the object in that the audience is cognizant and conscious of the 'absence' that is connoted by the 'substitution' or the transformational propensity of the condensation facility.

What is metaphoric becomes concretized as metaphoric through referral, since the artifact incorporates the measure of the transformational. It exhibits that the 'sign' also has a supplementary operation of its 'own' that is independent of the cultural formulation. That this is related to a notion of 'presence' that is desired when 'being' is barren of didactic facilities in the modern context for example. It was that which was related to articulating the role of the supplementary in the operation of the 'sign' in the context of archaic Man. In that since even the physical presence of the 'sign' was that which was comprised of an 'absence' in terms of articulating the 'meaning' it was possible to imbue it with, that what was pronounced was its supplementary aspect and the measure in the 'sign' to demonstrate its 'own' teleological implications. That the measure with which 'being' imbues 'meaning' in the structure of the 'sign', instigates deferral to both 'itself' and to an 'other'.

That with archaic Man the 'absence' of 'meaning' from the structure of the 'sign' was that which exhibited the measure in which he desired the 'presence'/presence of the didactic in the structure of the 'sign'. In the context of art, this applies to the extent that what is deferred in the structure of the 'sign' can also be demonstrated to be influenced by accretion, the epistemic, and the 'absence' that is connoted in the context of the art showcase.

Since the epistemic is contingent on the measure of accretion, this not only has implications for 'signs' in the unconscious, this is also the extent to which a condensation facility is a symbolic facility. That in the Lacanian structure of the conscious, it does not occupy the location of 'being' or 'self', rather it occupies the location of the symbolic subject and the propensity for deferral that this location is connoted with. In the context of art, this location is related to the transformational or 'substitution' inherent in 'being' since it occupies the location of the symbolic subject.

The extent to which 'being' is able to imbue 'meaning' on a 'sign' is crucial in the context of art. In that not only does it concretize the teleological measure of the epistemic and the implications of accretion. It also exhibits that the metaphoric structure of the 'sign' in the unconscious is symbolic. That what is symbolic has to be imbued with a measure of accretion. That the enunciative field or the initium, can exhibit has didactic implications or that through metaphysical facilities in a cultural dispensation in order to concretize the measure with which a 'sign' operates. These can be in the form of rituals and ablative exercises that demonstrate the desire for the didactic in 'being'. In that a condensation and displacement propensity in the 'sign' is concretized by repetition and deferral. Exhibiting that the supplementary aspect in the 'sign' is necessary for accretion by being conscious of the aspect of 'presence' and 'absence' in the structure of a 'sign'.

What necessitates art practice is that it discourses the measure with which the epistemic has assume institutional implications and connotations in the context of modernity. In that there has been instituted a context where knowledge operates as a condensation facility that concretizes logocentrism as the primary conduit in the relationship with the supplementary. Deconstruction has demonstrated that the essentialism that 'signs' are imbued within the logic of logocentrism, makes it possible for condensation facilities to be deferred to other condensation facilities. Not to state that deferral is not relevant, but that it in order to concretize a 'signs' didactic facility it has had to be imbued with a measure of purity, that the logic of the epistemic imbues with supplementary and supplementing propensities.

The discourse states that the epistemic is logical in the sense that in the context of modernity it is knowledge as a didactic tool that operates as a universal formative tool outside the context of the traditional social training. This in terms of addressing the notion of 'absence' and 'presence' that logocentrism and the pure and essentialist structure of the 'sign' is informed by. In that not only does knowledge demonstrate the supplementary operation of a 'sign' but it also exhibits that it is the measure with which the supplement has its 'own' supplementary or 'representational' aspect.

In the context of modernity it is the measure of the epistemic or knowledge as a metaphoric facility that imbues the logic of the 'initio' as a measure with which 'being' is able to implicate to the symbolic power. The 'presence' of the 'initio' is symbolic to the extent of the existential and the ontological. Not only is it concretized as a didactic facility, it also in the social context the measure with which it is concretized as a condensation facility. This is also the measure with which 'being' can demonstrate or exhibit that he or she is able to 'control' 'signs' in the unconscious, where a measure of their aggression operates at a 'conception' level, than a conceptual level.

The word 'conceptual' connotes accretion and the epistemic in terms of didactic notions, and the word 'conception' can connote the measure of the symbolic and supplementary deferral unlike the concrete notion of 'conceptual'.

That when the 'sign' is imbued with didactic or condensation facilities it is already always operational in the cultural dispensation and in the logic of logocentrism and epistemic as both originary and related to the unconscious. Art can through the logic of deferral demonstrate the measure in the 'sign' in the context of modernity has had to demonstrate its relationship to the supplement, not as just that which is supplementary but also as that which imbues the discourse of 'absence' and 'presence' with a measure of veracity and symbolic relevance in relation to a diverse multicultural community.

When the discourse utilizes the term 'veracity' it applies it in relation the notion of 'conception' or 'conceptual', where connotations of the symbolic operation relate to the epistemic and the condensation facility. That these pronounced the measure of the substitution that the ablative exercises sought to exhibit, that 'signs' are imbued with the logic of the logocentrism that is about what is metaphysical being related to the supplement. The word conception pronounces the location and context of the substitution and the ablative exercises. The word 'conceptual' connotes accretion and the referral propensity of the 'sign' in the conscious and the unconscious. A context where it has to operate with a measure of 'presence' and or 'absence' that characterizes the binary logic and the structure of infinite referral in the conception of deconstructionism.

If a 'sign' can operate with a measure of 'absence', then it is imbued with referral epistemic connotations. That this is also the measure with which the notion of 'conception' can imbued and influence within the structure of the 'sign' in order to concretize the context of the substitution. Art practice can exhibit that a 'sign' always already imbued with accrued epistemic implications that enable it to operate as a condensation facility. That in order for it to transform as a condensation facility it has to relinquish the very same condensation operation and conception that in one social or cultural paradigm imbues it with symbolic operations. In that when it relinquishes it imbues 'being' with symbolic implications, and when it appropriates 'meaning' then it is made symbolic by the supplementary and the supplement's operation in the structure of the 'sign'. Art can demonstrate that a 'sign' operates as a condensation facility to imbue 'being' with didactic implications and symbolic operations. That there is always already a measure of repetition that is imbedded in the initial processes of referral or imbuing with 'meaning' that at the context of appropriation a measure of deferral is required and exhibits the originary. That 'being' through the 'presence' of desire is conscious of the 'absence' of the didactic and is already always imbued with a measure of 'repetition' that has metaphysical connotations.

It is the 'presence' of desire in the cognitive spaces that imbues it with metaphysical connotations at one measure, but it is also the positivist sentiment of the 'presence' of desire that through temporal deferral 'being' can demonstrate is shared with the community. That as a tool for 'repetition' and 'presence' of the 'absence' requires exercises that correspond to the desire in the cognitive space, in order to not just imbue the 'new' 'presence' with palpable 'presence' in the cognitive space, but also to imbue this 'presence' with a relationship with intuitive connotations for the esoteric purposes of interpretation.

Interpretation is not only an exhibition of desire prior to the 'presence' of the didactic 'meaning', it is also a teleological devise for deferral, but also a measure for the representational aspect in the supplement. In the context of contemporary the measure of the esoteric interpretation has supplementary relevance in the sense that the symbolic power inculcates that in the context of the substitution there was an 'absence' in the encounter with diversity and the ethics of essentialism and 'purity' that inform the structure of the 'sign'.

Art not only exhibits the measure with which deferral is contingent on agency as it was in the context of archaic Man, but it is still that which is contingent on that which is about the measure of the supplement as a representational facility that discourses the measure of 'presence' and 'absence' as primarily that which are about the metonymic or the transformational. In that in the structure of diversity there is an 'absence' or a measure of didactic inconsistency, but it does not mean there is no longer any desire for that which is didactic. Rather it is embroiled in the discourse of what is symbolic in the 'sign' and the auto-affection it instigates in 'being'.

The structure of 'absence' in the context of modernity has been inculcated to be barren of the measure of the didactic or the formative. That the 'initio' is inculcated to be imbued with the necessary training and the propensity for desire for the didactic. Since it is 'absence' that instigates desire, in the context of modernity it is visual art practice that can demonstrate that this desire is originary and it enables implication to the symbolic power. That there is a measure of substitution that has ontological connotations that imbues the originary cultural location with both that which is subversive and reactionary to the symbolic power.

In relation to the notion of logocentrism, 'being' has had to exhibit a measure of desire for the didactic that has implications for 'origins' in the modern context. Since this discourse of 'origins' has connotations for training or the 'initio', it is this connotation for implication that imbue this training and the symbolic power with connotations for a representational and didactic aspect. Since 'being' is barren of the didactic training, the measure of 'presence' in a context where diversity and its connotations for 'absence' or what is binary to the symbolic power characterizes the cultural dispensation. It is also becomes that which is about how 'being' is independent from the symbolic power. The art object then becomes that which is about a measure of auto-affection that has connotations for 'being' relationship with the supplement and the symbolic power, but also the measure of the existential as a facility for the auto-didactic in that since the symbolic power requires auto-implication, this way the relationship is never about supplementing the 'presence' of the ethics and logic of modernity.

Dadaism and the episteme

The epistemic also has implications for the measure with which in the contemporary immediacy 'signs' can accrue and relinquish both 'meaning' and the metaphoric facility imbued on it by the didactic and formative strategies of the symbolic power. Maragoni (2004) cites Kristeva demonstrating the measure with which "...the materiality of individual elements ......cannot be excluded from the production of meaning and where processes are both systemic....and social" (Kristeva: Live Theory: 9). In a social context that is characterized by political and social upheaval this can be exhibited through the emergence of art movements like Dadaism. For example with the calamity that results in areas of conflict the security that is provided by the logic of the police force as both a didactic facility and a jurisdiction of the symbolic power results in this 'sign' as a social facility relinquishing its 'meaning' of protection and care. The emergence of socially specific didactic strategies in urban settings is a result of the symbolic power occupying and operating as the feminine or germinating principle that the logocentric logic concretizes as a didactic principle. The community has to be cognizant of this feminine principle both as a supplementary facility that justifies the 'presence' of the supplement, but also a means with which the community and its 'passive' location in relation to the symbolic power operates as a supplementary facility.

In a social context characterized by social and political upheaval, the community becomes imbued with a supplementary prerogative where they are responsible with moral and metaphysical connotations for signification implication of 'signs' in the 'new' in the cultural dispensation. This is not only a manifestation of the immediacy of the metonymic or displacement propensity of 'signs', but it is also the measure with which 'signs' of the community are demonstrated to be already always imbued with agency. This agency in the context in which Dadaism emerged was imbued with overt political connotations, where the dominant didactic facility was disseminated with 'negative' connotations, the art movement had to emerged with a "raucous skepticism about accepted values (Powel III et. Al, IX, 2005)".

In the context of advanced modernity didactic connotations are imbued with 'negative' implications related to the Deconstructionist notion of 'presence/absence' that characterizes the relationship between the structure of 'signs' and the symbolic power, but also the relationship the community builds with 'signs'. This measure of 'absence' becomes pronounce when signification is confronted with a context where 'signs' are contingent of their propensity to relinquish. This also demonstrates that the measure with which 'signs' operate, this propensity to relinquish is immediate, it is definitely not that which has implication for exhaustion. Where the boundary between its metaphysical connotations and implications is compounded even in urban advanced capitalism context by an immediate relationship with the supplement.

Maragoni (2004) states that this 'absence' becomes "reified"(9), or it becomes imbued with metaphysical connotations. This way the didactic connotations of the community as a 'sign' that is connected to symbolic power as a feminine principle that gestates the structure of 'signs', the community becomes a facility for manifestation or a metonymic facility instead of the physical structure that is traditionally purported to be manifestations or example of the 'presence' of formative strategies.

The symbolic power in the context of modernity is imbued with the propensity to demonstrate that 'signs' require a containing principle, where what is systematic and organized can be instituted and disseminated or manifested into the community. Since it also operates while being cognizant that it is 'absent' from the community, that it is not formulated within the community, it can be demonstrated that the community is an example of what Maragoni states is "textual signification" (2004: 9). In that the community is cognizant of itself as a 'sign' within the technical manifestations of the symbolic power, but in order to justify the measure with which it is related to the symbolic power in the urban setting it has to demonstrate its measure of implicating towards the symbolic power.

This implicating towards the symbolic power can be characterized as "the 'product' of an exceptional authorial mind" (2004:9), in the sense that Dadaism can be characterized as an inception of collective thinking in advanced capitalism where the urban setting was and is imbued with values that are communal. Like Freud's (De Ville: 3, 2009, http://repository.uwc.ac.za/xmlui/bitstream/handle/10566/302/DeVilleForceofLaw2009.pdf?sequence=4) nephew displaying strategies for independence during infancy, by relinquishing his attention from his toys attains the pleasure principle. That this psycho-analytic example is consistent with the symbolic power relinquishing its protection and care role in relation to the community, it can be detected it is a relationship based on 'negative' connotations and implications. The notion of the pleasure principle surfaces again in relation to the feminine principle as a maternal figure and supplementary to the symbolic power. This pleasure principle in the context of Dadaism was characterized by the "energy from the real prospect of revolution" (Gale, 120: 1997). De Ville states that Ernst Freud's nephew would take 'revenge' on his mother leaving him alone that in a metaphoric sense engage and induce metonymic manifestations in relation to his location as the subject of maternal care.

The community in the social and cultural upheaval that Dadaism emerged in can also be related to the measure with which the 'absence' of the supplement enables them to auto-reference in a metonymic and epistemic measure. Which imbues contemporary society with a relationship with 'signs' that has immediate transformational connotations. The immediacy that imbues 'signs' with a metonymic facility in a social context characterized by social upheaval, 'signs' can be detected to be imbued with political and ideological connotations that question the metaphysical implications and operations of the symbolic power. In that if the symbolic power is able to relinquish power in order to demonstrate power, as a condensation facility it can be detected that its structure as a metaphysical facility is imbued with an ambiguity that concretizes the aspect as a supplementary operator that is 'absent' than that which is 'present'.

That its relationship with the notion of the logocentric is purely strategic in that the metaphysical connotations of logocentrism are only metaphysical when power is challenged, and when as a feminine principle it auto-references than pronounce the measure with which it is related to the supplement.

Since logocentrism requires and is contingent on the actual presence/'presence' of its structures and its metaphysical intellectual implications. It can be detected that art movements are a manifestation of the pleasure principle (De Ville 2009), where the possibility for revolution and collective communal manifestation can be achieved.

The discourse of acknowledgments and distinctions can through the notion of hysteridence demonstrate that the relationship between the community and the symbolic power is imbued with a reciprocity that is contingent on the structure of supplementary operations of the symbolic power. Neither is independent; both are cognizant of their respective locations in relation to the metaphysical implications of logocentrism.

Chapter 5

Artifact, Archaic Man
and the Didactic

The discourse will demonstrate the measure with which the 'sign' is imbued with a relationship with the supplement. In order to do this it has to demonstrate the measure with which structures of signification in the context of modernity are imbued with ambiguous connotations. The discourse will demonstrate how even in the context of archaic man, it was the tool or artifact that help instigate a relationship with the supplement. That this is how the 'sign' or tool can be a facility that enables 'being' to interrogate the moral implications of the essentialism in modernity's conception of the 'sign'.

The discourse has to demonstrate the measure with which archaic Man and contemporary art practice are interested in a measure of signification that has a relationship with the unconscious. It then becomes significant for the discourse to demonstrate the measure with which the 'sign' is able to relate to the community by imbuing the 'sign' through signification with symbolic 'meaning'.

By incorporating Jung's understanding of the artist's social or transcendental role, the discourse will attempt to demonstrate how the 'sign' is able to concretize the capacity of the 'sign' of the community to be organically imbued with supplementary connotations. That this in the context of modernity can be exhibited by art practice, how there can be a didactic consistency between the community and the symbolic power through the structure of signification.

The chapter will demonstrate the measure with which 'signs' in the context of the community primarily operate with metonymic connotations and implications. It will also demonstrate the measure with the community, since the context of the substitution has been severed from its relationship with the supplement through implicating towards the symbolic power, with austere implications.

The discourse in this chapter has to demonstrate the measure with which the 'sign' has connotations for relinquishing in relation to the symbolic power and the supplement. It will make a comparison between the contemporary operation of 'signs' and archaic Man in order to demonstrate how the symbolic power and the community are contingent on the accretion that is necessary in the epistemic.

The chapter also seeks to demonstrate the measure with which art practice demonstrates how the transformation or substitution capacity of the 'sign' has to be imbued with existential connotations in order to be concretized with the logic of the positivism that informs logocentrism or the supplement. The discourse also seeks to demonstrate the measure with which 'signs' are necessary for deferral, in terms of the deconstructionist notion of a phenomenology of deferral, with its implications for that which is to come and significance of accretion in the structures of signification.

Of Archaic Man and the didactic

In the context of 'being' 'presence' of 'self' is not about justifying the 'presence' of the supplement. In that the 'performance' that is necessary in deferring to the supplement especially in the context of archaic man, had connotations for a formative intellectual tool. A tool whose existential implications demonstrated the metonymic operation of the 'self' as more than just a symbolic didactic facility, especially in the context of the community. What was necessary was to establish the metaphoric source that justified and concretized the metaphoric location and operation of the 'being' or 'self' with the primary didactic function in the community. That 'being' is always already conscious of 'self' as a referral facility who is contingent on what is symbolic to cultivate and invoke intellectual processes, for learning and socio cultural orientation. The necessity of the artifact or object to be imbued with 'meaning' extends beyond the notion of the didactic and its relationship with the supplement. It also concretizes the metaphysical location and operation of 'being' in that it provides a facility for 'being' to differentiate self from self, but also to differentiate the object from itself.

That this not only renders the object metaphysical, but it imbues the notion of 'meaning' of the object both with deferral implications and auto-referential connotations. That the object has to operate as a both a 'signifier' and the 'signified', not just for metaphoric and metonymic implications in the unconscious and the conscious. The 'sign' or object can exhibit that it is impossible to desire in 'presence'. The artifact can exhibit that the supplement imbues the 'sign' with metonymic or displacement propensities that can demonstrate that 'meaning' is not just a collective endeavor. It is also that which induces discourse for the fullest measure of presence. That the object instigates discourse not just as that which is a cultural orientation facility, it is also that which can exhibit that desire has teleological implications in relation to the unconscious and the supplement.

In the context of modernity, since the didactic logic can or has accounted for the 'presence' of 'absence' in the form of the diversity that informs the community. It is also that which requires what is positivist or what is witnessable to inform the didactic connotation or implication. That this way it becomes impossible to establish grounds upon which a 'sign' can operate with transformational connotations, in that what is concretized is its metaphoric or symbolic connotations.

The symbolic power in the context of modernity inculcates itself through the facility of the 'initio' as a 'representer' of the community and the symbolic power than as a facility that 'signifies' towards it in relation to the supplement. In the context of modernity it is the measure of agency in 'being' that enables what is teleological in the context of logocentrism to be imbued with pure and essentialist discourse. In that the 'absence' in the context of modernity and the 'absence' in the context of archaic Man are differentiated by the measure of accretion. Not its teleological implications, but its connotations and implications for relinquishing in the structure of the 'sign' where in the context of archaic man, he or she had to relinquish the discourse of 'absence' in relation to the supplement and the 'sign'. In the context of modernity the measure of 'absence' is related to relinquishing the 'presence' in the structure of the 'sign' as informed by the rural and feudal context. That art practice through infinite referral can demonstrate the measure with which accretion and relinquishing exhibit how it is impossible to desire through 'presence'. Part of the art object's teleological's function is the desire with which an audience desires consumption and the realization of that desire. Not only is the discourse of art the 'absence' of the didactic measure in the 'being' or the community, but part of its collective paradigm discourses the metaphoric and metonymic implications in the context of the substitution.

That if there was a measure of 'absence' in the context of the substitution what was related to that which is didactic, it could be related to the logocentric in that there was an 'absence' in its struc-

ture than in 'being'. In 'being' since he or she can never fully account for the fullest measure of presence even through the facility
of the cultural formulation, there is bound to be a desire for the
didactic inclinations in the formulations of an 'other', and that the
metonymic operations of a 'sign' can exhibit in the context of the
substitution that the logocentric was absent/'absent'.

In relation to that which is didactic, the notion of 'presence' even
in the context of a substitution has implications and connotations
for the supplementary. That if there is a 'presence' or presence it is
impossible to desire, in that desire has already been realized. In the
context of the substitution in the processes of modernity desire was
also that which was 'present' through the 'absence' of the universal
didactic ethic but also what is universal about ethics and processes
of acquiring wealth. The facility of the 'initio' and its implications
for the logocentric are that which are inculcated and deferred as
'absent' as a supplementary facility to the community. This way it
can be inculcated as a supplementary facility for the logocentric supplementing the community. The 'initio' can be deferred
to the community as much as the supplement could defer to the
community and the 'being' responsible for invoking it in archaic
man, but 'being' in the context of the modernity operates with the
pure and essentialist structure that is auto-referential and autocratic.

Art practices just like in the context of archaic Man can exhibit
that in order for 'signs' to stop deferring structures of concretization
related to what been accrued in the structure of that relevant
'sign' have to be invoked, in that essentialism can be characterized
as self-referential. This self-referentialism of the 'initio' is significant to the extent that what is metaphysical becomes embroiled in
more than just the discourse of 'presence' but it also becomes incorporated in how the 'presence' can be refuted and inculcated as
'absent'.

Part of the reason why the symbolic power refutes the 'presence'
of the didactic in the community is to concretize its own representational aspect in relation to the supplement. That through the
facility of the logocentrism enables to concretize the binary or dichotomous logic. Art and the discourse of deconstructionism are
facilities in the context of modernity that seek to demonstrate that
what is metaphysical in the relationship between 'being' and the
symbolic power or between the community and the symbolic power is reserved for the logocentric and its relationship with the supplement. That this relationship characterizes the passive location

of the context of the community and part of the teleological implications of art practice that seek to demonstrate that what is didactic in the community is disseminated through positivist
or witnessable connotations. Not to diminish the metaphysical
operation of 'signs' but rather to privilege what is positivist
and witnessable in the structures of the 'sign'.

Art practice can exhibit that that which allows the logocentrism to
be possible has teleological implications for the symbolic power.
Related to the notion of the discursive or the production of knowledge rather than that which allows knowledge to have a relationship with the supplement in the context of 'being' and the community. In the sense that art practice has a relationship with the supplement that is organic to the community and cultivating of that
which is didactic for example. That this is also the measure which
exhibits that 'meaning' in the structure of 'signs' can be related to
the supplement. That modernity has inculcated that the subversive
side of the binary does not possess a metaphysical aspect without
the auspices of the symbolic power.

The artifact in the context of archaic Man, the object was 'barren'
of 'meaning', in that 'being' had not imbued it with metaphysical
connotations, it was the supplement that provided the primary
didactic facility. Its mystery lay in the didactic measure or discourse of that which was elusive about 'presence', he or she unders-
tood that they were a conduit of the 'presence' of the supplement.
That 'meaning' provided a didactic facility and what
was originary about agency in relation to 'being' differentiating himself from himself, and differentiating the supplement from 'itself'.

'Being' was conscious of desire as a deferral facility towards the
supplement, that through instinct the supplement as 'sign' was
susceptible to metonymic implications and connotations where 'it'
could defer to 'being' and 'being' could defer to the supplement in
order to imbue the desire for the didactic with a deferral facility. The object operated not as just means for differentiation, but it
was also a facility for discourse, to concretize the supplement and
instigate the supplementary in its own operation. The object provided the facility for 'presence' its own physical presence, but as a
'presence' of 'meaning' through its malleability it was a manifestation for what was instinctive about desire. That the object already
had a supplementary aspect or a representational aspect, it was the
didactic in 'being' that even through the symbolic presence of 'being', the meaning of this 'presence' needed discourse but also the

measure and means to account or instigate discourse for the fullest measure of presence.

The symbolic power in the context of modernity instigates discourse through the ethics of presence and positivism, for the fullest measure of presence through the production of knowledge and the discursive. Even though it accounts for the didactic they cannot account for the fullest measure of presence, it can only account for the symbolic operation of the facilities that account for the didactic in a cultural dispensation, since they are also contingent on cultural formulations to account for them.

Art practice in the context of modernity can exhibit that positivism is a didactic facility, part of the structures of 'meaning' in the structure of the 'sign' in a measure that seeks to exhibit that the facility of the binary concretizes 'absence' in one aspect of the dichotomy. An 'absence' that is barren of the accretion inculcated and incorporated in the didactic structure of the epistemic and sovereignty from the rural to the urban setting. Art practice can exhibit that the play of substitution in the structure of the 'sign' in the context of modernity is impossible in that it is 'manufactured' away from his or her 'being' therefore barren of the agency and means to articulate auto-affection that is about relating him or her to the supplement.

The measure with which the 'being' in the context of modernity is 'barren' of the didactic can only be detected through the deferral processes of the symbolic power. Deferral art practice can demonstrate is not possible unless there is a measure of 'presence' both abstract and physical. Not only does this render the measure with which the symbolic power disseminates it is also subject to representational facility that is fundamental to concretizing positivist and discursive formulations. It also concretizes that both the community and the symbolic power are contingent on the supplement for concretizing discourse of presence/'presence' and absence/'absence'.

This way the symbolic power cannot be privileged more than the 'presence' or 'absence' of the didactic in the context of the community. Art also seeks to exhibit that if the community requires a relationship with the supplement through a conduit other than 'being' or the community then the facility that makes what is didactic in the context of modernity possible is contingent on the facility that makes its presence possible which is the cultural formulation.

In the context of modernity the artifact cannot loose its relationship with the supplement, in that if it does then 'being' has lost his or her relationship with the supplement. The cultural formulation cannot usurp the originary agency that is within 'being' in that it cannot demonstrate itself with accretion facilities and it cannot account for the location of 'self' as imbued with substitution facilities.

Art practice can exhibit that the measure of substitution in the context of modernity has demonstrated that 'being' or 'self' is also a 'sign' that has accretion facilities. That these facilities require the positivist evidence in the context of modernity due to the 'absence' that the symbolic power can exhibit is lacking. That which is lacking has relevance for the ontological, art practice can also exhibit since it is in the abstract spaces of the conscious and the unconscious, accretion, deferral and the symbolic role of the epistemic are tools with which 'being' can still relate to the supplement and still be subject to the symbolic power.

This way his or her relationship with the supplement will not be structured in a measure that seeks to 'perform' roles or a role that imbues the notion of substitution with measures that are consistent with the contemporary formulation. In that 'roles' are symbolic of the relationship with the symbolic power and the 'being' and what is originary about agency is symbolic of the didactic nature of his or her relationship with the supplement. That the notion of a substitution enables a 'sign' to operate with epistemic and accrued connotations, this way the 'sign' instigates auto-affection through originary agency.

Modernity and its positivist ethics seeks to exhibit that 'being' has to desire in 'presence' or in person in order to assume his or her symbolic role. This way the 'absence' is not what makes 'presence' possible or impossible but is a permanent condition in the diverse structure of the community as a 'sign' with a relationship with the symbolic power. Art practice can exhibit that even when the didactic ethic is 'present' in a symbolic measure in the 'sign' of 'being', the facility of implication to the symbolic power renders him or her a subject of the symbolic power than a supplementary facility of the symbolic power. The supplementary operation can exhibit that there is a measure of agency in 'being'. That auto-affection and the supplement are embroiled in a deferral relationship that is symbolic of the fullest measure of presence and the operation of the supplement that has didactic implications in the context of 'being'.

Art practice in the context of modernity has imbued the accretion of the 'sign' with an 'absence' that is contingent on that which is didactic in the structure of the symbolic power. Art practice can exhibit that it is the supplement that has an ephemeral structure and the cultural formulation that has accretion and epistemic connotations.

That this not only imbues 'being' with a propensity for agency but it demonstrates that logocentrism enjoys a metaphysical privilege more than the 'sign' of the community. That this is also the space where the spiritual institution is 'barren' of the didactic measure in relation to the processes of modernity in its structure even though it is imbued with epistemic connotations.

In that that which can refute what is metaphysical in the structure of a 'sign' is also that which also has metaphysical implications. Art practice can demonstrate that what is metaphysical in the structure of the symbolic power usurps the measure and facility of agency in 'being'. In that art can demonstrate that 'being' has his or her own 'representational' aspect that has epistemic and originary connotations from the rural context therefore 'being' is 'barren' of the measure of the essentialist didactic logic of the symbolic power.

In the context of archaic Man, the object with the 'meaning' that was attributed or deferred to it was that which, in order to render 'meaning' didactic it had to demonstrate the measure in the structure of the 'sign' to related to the supplement. That this was the measure with which 'presence' of the physical and abstract 'sign' due to their 'independence' from 'being' assumed supplementary or operational connotations. The object in the context of archaic man was that which could exhibit the symbolic location of 'being' or that he or she was a conduit between the supplement and 'meaning'. That through desire this is the measure with which deferral instigated discourse and 'meaning'. Desire was the manifestation of agency or the catalyst of intention, that this was the measure with which what is supplementary was structured or informed the 'sign'. The supplement was the instinctive 'absence' of the didactic or 'meaning' in the 'sign', but that 'signs' had 'patrons' or supplementary influences towards the supplement exhibited the measure with which agency had and still has originary symbolic significance.

Artifact, the breach and cerebrinity

The artifact is the facility with which the community instigates discourse of the metaphysical even in the context of modernity. In that accretion and the epistemic allows through the facility of relinquishing 'meaning', even the operation of a 'sign', the 'sign' to have a relationship with the supplement. The symbolic power in the context of modernity attributes 'signs' with rigid and austere structures that are not malleable even in the social context, or with its encounter with the community or community member. The rigid structure of the 'sign' then can be detected operates as means which concretizes the metaphysical operation and location of the symbolic power.

It becomes significant to establish the metaphysical location of the symbolic power in the context of advanced modernity in that not only does the community rely on it for didactic implications. The community also relies on it to articulate its own epistemic location in relation to it and in relation to itself. Art practice while being cognizant of the austere structure of 'signs' in the modernist context rises to concretize the metaphysical operation of 'signs'. In that even though 'signs' are austere in the context of art practice they occupy the dichotomous location in relation to the symbolic power that is traditionally purported to be the organic and submissive. That art practice is contingent on the 'absence' that is 'present' in the structure of the 'sign' to emphasizes the Deconstructionist notion of differance where the 'signs' are perpetually referring and accumulating 'meaning'.

In the context in which Dadaism emerged it became significant for the art that was produced to be cognizant that the symbolic power has relinquished its location and metaphysical operation as a primary didactic facility in the cultural global dispensation. That this also demonstrated what the discourse of acknowledgements and distinctions designates is the hysteridentical relationship between the community and the symbolic power. In that they both characterized a structure in which the 'sign' has a relationship with the supplement, where 'presence' and 'absence' are imbued with a symbiotic relationship. Where the Deconstructionist notion of arche-writing discerned a breach of communication between 'signs' themselves but also between the community and the symbolic power. The breach in a political and social upheaval becomes characterized by violence and the symbolic power relinquishing its didactic and metaphysical relationship with the supplement. As a supplementary operation it merely auto-references, emphasizes its location as the contained feminine principle that disseminates formative and didactic strategies to the community.

In relation to archaic Man, modernity relies on the symbolic power for didactic and metaphysical operations and connotations in relating to 'signs'. These are not only related to the measure with which the community is contingent on the ritualistic measure the symbolic power establishes its power to the community, but for archaic Man, it was his cerebrinous and intellectual illumination relating to the object or 'sign'. Modern society in order to establish the didactic relationship with the symbolic power has to witness through ablative exercises the marked historic points of change in the social structure, through which the metaphysical implications and connotations of the symbolic power are established.

Through the practice of art, the supplementary operation of the community can be detected, in that not only do the ablative exercises that establish its passive location related to measure of infinite referral that Deconstructionism purports informs the structure of 'signs'. It demonstrates that in the context of modernity the breach of communication in the structure of 'signs' is exacerbated by social upheaval contexts, they are also worsened by the logic in the symbolic power that is contingent on the epistemic conception of logocentrism. That is the symbolic power relinquishes its power through word that is in the same manner in which it appropriates it. That this power becomes pronounced as logocentric in contexts of social and cultural upheaval is demonstrative of the feminine principal operation. The feminine principal operation seeks to compensate for the breach of communication between 'signs', but since the breach is organic both the symbolic power and the community are cognizant of it. Both are cognizant of it. Art practice by occupying the submissive location in the relationship with the symbolic power, is able to demonstrate the measure with which it is related to itself. Through the 'sign' and overt implication of temporal referencing:

> *"....the artist is the exact opposite of an official*
> *in so far a specifically artistic psychology is more*
> *collective than personal in character.... The artist*
> *is not a person endowed with free will who seeks*
> *his own ends...but an artist is a 'man' in a higher*

sense – he is 'collective man' – a vehicle
and moulder of the unconscious psychic life of
mankind" (Jung, C.G, "The Collected Works: Volume Fifteen: The Spirit in Man, Art and Literature" , pp. 101: 1966)

The notion of hysteridence is also informed by the infinite reference structure of 'signs', but since it emphasizes what is formative
and didactic it is able to demonstrate the measure with which there
is a common goal between the didactic strategies of the symbolic
power and the community. That these didactic goals are rendered
by the breach of communication in the structure of
'signs' hysteridentical, in that not only does the negativity that
structures the relationship with symbolic power also that which
informs and structures of 'signs' in the context of the community, it
is also that which emphasizes an epistemic and teleological implication.

The role of art practice and the artist demonstrates that these implications have a relationship with the supplement or the collective
unconscious. Where the symbolic power operates as a feminine
principle that guides the community in a teleological measure. Hysteridence presupposes psychological and cognitive strategies related to the formative strategies in an immediate sense,
where in the social context it is the negative logic that demonstrates
an individual's sense of psychological balance when relating to the
symbolic power. In the context of art practice this negative formative strategy becomes exposed for its austere rigidity in that not only
does it pronounce the epistemic and teleological implications, it is
the only social facility with which the relationship between the
symbolic power and the community is recognized for its organic
symbiotic operation as a manifestation and containing principles in
their respective 'roles'.

The notion of hysteridence caters and articulates how the 'fullest
measure of presence' in a cultural dispensation is related to the
supplement in a metaphysical and immediate measure. In that not
only do the 'signs' emphasize 'absence' in their structure, but they
also emphasize that the 'absence' of the supplement has an epistemic relationship with the contemporary symbolic power. That
the ablative exercises that instituted the current structure of 'signs'
had foundations that are 'negative'. What renders them hysteri-

dentical is the relationship with the supplement that is based on the 'absence' or what is unwitnessable structure of the feminine principle. Since 'signs' lack a structure or organized form in the feminine aspect of the supplement and the community does not have a jurisdiction over the feminine principle of the symbolic power. Art practice with implications for order and social creativity, emphasizes diversity in the community but also that the community has its supplementary relationship with the supplement independent of the symbolic power.

This can be demonstrated on the necessary referral in the structure of 'signs' in the context of modernity. That this is pronounced in the operation of 'signs' in the ablative exercises that marked transitions, where the 'absence' that was emphasized by the substitution was also that which informed the logic behind the negativity that structures didactic and formative strategies in the context of modernity.

In contrast to archaic man, with his cerebrinous encounter with the object as a facility that induces spiritual and intellectual investigation, which is a moment that can be related to the 'manufacturing' of the unconscious through accretion and the operation of 'absence' or insubstantiality that 'meaning' was imbued within that context. Jung's analyses that man as artist occupies a higher collective consciousness imbues the discourse of the artifact in the modern context being with imbued with spiritual connotations. In that even at the inception of accretion in archaic man, the 'presence' of 'absence' informed the structure of the 'sign'. It can be deduced that even for prehistoric man the presence/'presence' of the 'sign' whose function had a revelatory pragmatism related to the item and the measure with which it accrued pyscho-social 'meaning'. The spiritual implications of an object can be related to the measure with they induce a cerebrinous relationship with the 'being'. Where its epistemic accretion can be related to the measure with which pragmatism and repetition are necessary and significant.

The notion of the breach can also be related to Jung's notion of man as artist in that the inconsistency that is detected can also be related to the measure with which 'higher collective consciousness' is imbued with characteristics of service and its implications of chance or universal choreography. In that not only did the artist and the 'being' with higher collective consciousness in the context of archaic man occupy and 'perform' a similar service in relation to the 'sign' or object, they were also contingent on the operation of 'absence' in the structure of the 'sign' in to induce a cerebrinous experience.

Chapter 6

Performance art and the Immediacy of the social context

This chapter will seek to demonstrate the measure with which the symbolic power also has a relationship with the supplement, that it is contingent upon it to concretize a relationship with the 'signs' through the facility of the initium. The discourse also has to demonstrate the measure with which the community and the 'being' have a relationship with the supplement that is independent of the symbolic power.

It will demonstrate how the symbolic power has a facility with which to subjugate 'being' and that this facility impedes the manner in which 'being' can establish a relationship with the symbolic power. The discourse will demonstrate the significance of being conscious of this facility, and the measure with which it can instigate a relationship with the unconscious through the facility of the archetypes. Citing Hill (1992) the discourse will also compare this facility from the symbolic power with the mastering implications of the performance artist. That being conscious of a relationship with the unconscious provides the performance artist with a facility for choreography imbued with an organic veracity. This veracity also has connotations for the measure with which 'signs' in the context of the unconscious are imbued with essentialist connotations and implications.

This way the discourse can demonstrate how the symbolic power is contingent on auto-differentiation logic within the structure of its own 'signs'. In relation to the community it establishes as a didactic logic, how the community is conscious of its own distance from the symbolic power.

This chapter seeks to demonstrate the teleological implications of performance art in the context of modernity, how it is also a measure with which the community establishes a relationship with the supplement.

The chapter also compares the 'signs' of the community and the symbolic power, how they operate, that one operates with feminine connotations and the other operates with masculine or creative connotations respectively. That this helps detect the structure and implication of the 'signification' or the 'signifier' in the context of modernity.

This way it will attempt to demonstrate the measure with which what is hysteridenctical is discoursed by the facility of teleological implications in performance art. That it achieves this by 'repeating' the social spectacle as that which informs its choreography. Which has relevance for both what is 'negative' and 'positive' in the social structure.

Of performance art and the social context

In the context of modernity art practice is necessary due to the measure of the 'absence' of the didactic in the context of relation-ship between the community and the symbolic power. It is also an exhibition of the measure of the originary and the jurisdiction of agency in the context of 'being'. That this is also the measure with which 'being' in order to demonstrate an individual relationship with the supplement can account for him or herself.

To implicate subsumes that 'being' is conscious of his or her rela-tionship with the supplement. That the symbolic apparatus or cul-tural formulation also has a limited relationship with the supple-ment. That the cultural formulation has implications for a represen-tational aspect in the structure of the supplement. In the context of modernity art practice can be imbued with moralistic or ethical connotations even without the didactic training of the symbolic power not being incorporated in the structure of the 'sign'.

In the context of modernity what is didactic has been rendered or inculcated as 'absent' by the symbolic power in order to exhibit that the facility of the 'initio' enables 'being' to auto-differentiate. That the measure of the 'absence' has existential connotations, and therefore characteristic and consistent with the isolated isolations of the originary cultural formulations from the rural to the urban context.

Since the facility of 'initio' has implications for auto-affection or the processes of the existential, 'being' or 'self' as a 'sign' related to the facility of the supplement, cannot operate with a measure of 'absence' in order to inculcated or be concretized as that whose structure is informed by what is essentialist or 'pure'.

In order for the 'sign' to operate as essentialist it has to have established a relationship with the supplement, there has to be evidence of its supplementary accretion and operation, in the form of its role in the ritual and ablative exercises in the particular cultural context.

Art practice can exhibit that the epistemic is always already informed and implicated in the context of the substitution. That the 'sign' requires exercises related to its accretion and its relationship with the supplement in order to concretize or demonstrate how it relinquished 'meaning'. For example if we take the refuge or a home as a 'sign' that has accrued 'meaning' from archaic man, its didactic implications were that which accrued not just as a utilitarian symbol but also the measure in which it is related to the supplement as a didactic tool. If a tool relinquishes 'meaning' it has implications for desire and its instinctive connotations in 'being', in order to acquire 'new' 'meaning'.

The ritualistic measure with which art practice has manifested itself in the context modernity, or in the twentieth century especially, is that it is consistent with the ablative exercises that have characterized the contexts of the substitution from the rural to the urban context. The extent to which 'being' cannot instigate an ablative exercise without the auspices of the community or an audience, both for deferral purposes but also for accretion and relinquishing purposes is that he or she is symbolic in an auto-referential and cultural formation measure. The extent to which performance art is existential is also a manifestation of desire as a facility for conscious orientation. It is symbolic of the condensation facility that the symbolic power inculcates to be the 'absence' that characterizes the context of modernity.

Lippard (1990) writes about the emergence of performance art in the 1970's and 1980's in North American, with its strong influence of Black women who emphasized and demonstrated a consistency with the necessity of the ablative exercise in the context of modernity. She states that for performance artists it became significant to identify with "...land, place, family (and therefore history) begins with the body, so storytelling (for) performance artist in particular have their senses tuned to the rhythms, gestures, accents, local color and climates where they came up or came out....Black women especially young women (where a manifestation that) performance art came into its own with the beginnings of the feminist movement around 1970 and women have led its ranks" (91-92). Which explicates the measure with which context and location in the ablative exercise and in the context of performance art have a consistency related to the veracity of social contexts where differentiation in the operation and structure of 'signs' is necessary.

The transcendental measure in the structure of the 'sign' she explicates is pronounced, the performance operating as that which "reclaims ….a connection with the traditional African nuances of his or her task, whereby the art object was created to be used as part of the grand performance- i.e. ritual that addressed the needs of an entire community" (91-93).

This is what renders what is 'metaphysical' about performance art to be immediate and accessible to the artist, in that it is the measure with which it imbues the audience and the artist him or herself with a displacement facility that is about auto-differentiation and the measure of 'play' in the performance.

The significance of performance art in the context of modernity emanates from the symbolic power's didactic strategy that 'signs' cannot account for the fullest measure of presence in the cultural dispensation. Since the performance artist is discoursing the measure of 'absence' of the didactic, presence in the performance piece is about what is symbolic about accretion of the 'sign' as 'being' and its relationship with 'being'. In that auto-affection in the context of performance art has connotations for the measure of the heterogeneity that is necessary in the social context, and in the ontological space.

In that between 'being' and the symbolic power there is an 'absence' that is imbued with originary connotations that is related to the supplement through the facility of the logocentrism. 'Being' becomes a 'sign' that has to be appropriated into a cultural formulation instead of being an entity that is symbolic of the 'presence' of the supplement. Performance art can also be related to the condensation facility in the collective unconscious as being crucial in the context of modernity as a didactic facility. In that to inculcate that there is a didactic 'absence' in the cultural dispensation is to inculcate that what is epistemic has relevance for logocentrism.

There are logical implications in the logocentric strategy that state that there is no didactic principle in the context of the substitution, through the diversity that characterized it, but also through the 'absence' of a positivist and witnessable didactic facility between cultures. Relating this 'absence' to knowledge not only imbues it with metaphysical connotations, but it also renders the discourse of the exegetic to be that which has implications for the 'absence' that characterized the context of the substitution. The significance of performance art discoursing and incorporating the social context or 'repeating' public spectacle in the performance, exhibits the consistency between the ablative immediacy of the substitution and the absence that characterized the symbolic power disseminating itself. It is also that which pronounces the measure of auto-biography in the narrative of the substitution or modernity. Where 'being' has to auto-differentiate in order to articulate what is epistemic and symbolic about accretion in the structure of the 'sign'. That this also has implications for the discourse of origins as both stable and malleable in the context of modernity.

The performance has to be consistent with the measure of the immediacy in the social context in that it exhibits auto-affection to be an autonomous operation in 'being'. That if what is didactic has to appropriated, performance art can exhibit that the dualism between 'being' and the symbolic power is hysteridentical. In that if 'being' has to 'tell' the auto-biography of his or her differentiation from the identity orientation and facilities of the symbolic power, and the symbolic power can demonstrate that 'being' is barren of this didactic auto-biography. This not only concretizes the ambiguous relationship between 'being' and the symbolic power, but it also concretizes the measure of negation that is implied in the notion of hysteridence.

What is hysteridentical is comprised of the orientation facilities imbedded in the symbolic power and the accrued notions of 'signs' incorporated in the structure of the originary. The symbolic power is cognizant of the fact that 'signs' have been accrued into the context of modernity. In that in relation to the supplement 'signs' must maintain their supplementary operation in order to concretize the facility of the logocentrism as a deferral facility but also a measure that instigates discourse about the metaphysical.

In the context of modernity and in the structure of the teleological implications of art the exegetic and the metaphysical are that which have implications for the measure of the didactic. Since the community is barren of the didactic, performance art and art practice are that which emerge out of the originary desire for the didactic in collective conscious and unconscious.

In the context of modernity the temporal operation of the 'sign' is the primary measure of the didactic in the cultural dispensation. This way the facility of the 'initio' can be imbued with the universalism that is connoted by the temporal instead of the particular didactic connotations of the sacred.

Performance art seeks to exhibit that the measure of the didactic can be barren of the metaphysical, in that the metaphysical concretizes the condensation facility in the conscious and the unconscious to be that which is deferred and related to the supplement. In order for a 'sign' to operate as didactic facility it has to be established as a metaphoric or condensation 'sign', this way it can be demonstrated to have a relationship with the supplement. What is supplementary about it can also be deduced in its processes of accretion. Accretion is also that which can be demonstrated to be the measure with which 'being' appropriates an orientation facility, that the pronouncing of the temporal is a measure of the extent of accretion and relinquishing the 'sign' has gone through.

The immediacy of the social context under the auspices of modernity imbues the 'sign' with as much accretion and relinquishing purposes. In that the 'being' with the dominant 'initio' is imbued with the power to enable the 'sign' to relinquish power but not its 'meaning' or its relationship with the supplement. The measure of the originary auto-biography in the social context has relevance with expression, not as performance but as a means to exhibit power and the originary jurisdiction. This is not to state that 'being' has to perform for the sake of exhibiting that he or she has a relationship with the supplement. It is a manifestation of desire in 'being' and the measure of how 'signs' are in constant flux in terms of deferral and communication.

What is hysteridentical in the context of modernity is the inconsistency within the structure of the 'sign' in that since is 'barren' of exegetic implications. Rather it is imbued with essentialist connotations, it does not provide 'being' with a differentiation facility that is related to the supplement. The 'being' seeks to exhibit that the condensation facility can enable 'being' to demonstrate in the social context and in the context of the performance art. That he or she is part of the processes of deferral that the deconstructionist notion of difference has sought to exhibit is part of the infinite operation of the 'sign'.

Performance art can also demonstrate that if the symbolic power has its own supplementary aspect in the facility of logocentrism.

Then it can be deduced that it is necessary for 'being' to auto-differentiate in relation to the didactic facility of the symbolic power. Since 'being' is present, he or she has to differentiate him or herself from the 'absence' that the symbolic power purports characterizes the cultural dispensation. Since there is an 'absence' of the didactic in the relationship between 'being' and the symbolic power, art practice is invested in the processes of auto-affection or self relating that imbue the relationship between 'being' and the symbolic power with a measure of autobiography.

Immediacy in the social context implies the measure with which power between 'beings' is closer and distant from the representational aspect of the supplement. That which is hysteridentical in the social context is implicated through the disintegration or exhaustion of the moment of interaction. That which is exhausted is the 'absence' that is implicated and connoted by the 'presence' of the 'absence' in 'being'. Performance art can exhibit that this exhaustion of the moment has connotations for the measure with which 'being' can differentiate him or herself from both the traditional social training and the measure of the 'absence' that is inculcated to characterize the didactic.

Art practice is also a facility that can exhibit that this measure of 'absence' is 'present' or present, with positivist manifestations like communities on the periphery of the symbolic center, the prevalence of poverty and the community being characterized by a diversity of peoples and cultures. Since the supplement has its own supplementary or representational aspect the 'absence' that the symbolic power relates to the community and to the individual 'being' has connotations for deferral or 'instruction' about the didactic disposition within the context or the moment. Performance art has connotations for auto-affection and presence within the moment of the performance. In that the performance has connotations for the present in terms of the unfolding of time, the symbolic location of 'being' in relation to the supplement, the performance highlights the symbolic subject as that which is the discourse of the performance or the character.

Performance art is also a facility that enables 'being' to self relate or auto-differentiate, that this is also the measure with which the 'being' is able to exhibit the historical veracity of the context of modernity. That in the context of 'being' what is symbolic has connotations for accretion in a measure that can also exhibit this propensity in 'being' for heterogeneity, or that which can be characterized as hysteridentical is what characterizes the relationship with the symbolic power.

In that art is a social practice that also incorporates the ethical and non-ethical aspects of the cultural dispensation, in the forms they are devised in the context of modernity, and that when they are related to the epistemic and accretion they have relevance to logocentrism and its relationship with the supplement.

The hysteridentical has implications for both negative and positive connotations, since 'being' is a symbolic entity in his or her relationship with 'signs'. Performance art emerged to concretize this symbolic operation, to exhibit that the 'absence' that the symbolic power attributes to the location of the community has connotations for the didactic and that the community cannot be barren of a relationship with the supplement. The existential implications of performance art are that which have connotations for the measure with which 'being' implicates him or herself towards the symbolic power. That the extent to which this implication is contingent on agency and power is pronounced by the measure of 'absence' and its didactic implications. 'Being' and the community are that which appropriate the didactic, supplementary connotations of the 'absence', through agency and originary power. 'Being' and community are cognizant of their own relationship with the representational aspect of the supplement that is beyond the operation of the symbolic power as a cultural formulation.

This relationship between 'being' and the representational aspect of the supplement has connotations for the measure with which power and its operation are symbolic in relation to 'signs' and the cultivation of 'meaning' through the originary desire. Performance art is a manifestation of the desire for the didactic within the cultural formulation that accommodates 'absence' as a didactical foundation that has condensation implications. Art practice in general renders this condensation facility as discourse that seeks to demonstrate that 'signs' and their displacement propensities imbue their relationship with 'being' with differentiation facilities.

The notion of hysteridence is defined by difference, difference of identity and formative implications, differences of cultural and economic foundations or backgrounds. Hysteridence is also that which has implication for similarities in the context of modernity. Similarities in ethics of security, similarities in the values of community and an implicit appropriation of the measure of 'absence' that characterizes the relationship between the community and the symbolic power that is accepted in all aspects of the cultural dispensation. Similarities in the ethics of wealth with their implications for immediacy and consumption. Hysteridence is an organic manifestation that is a result of the inconsistencies that essentialist structure 'signs' operate with. Where power is discernible as diffused throughout the community in an originary and organic measure regardless of background or class.

Performance art as hysteridentical

In the context of modernity with its hyper-individualized formative and didactic strategies the logic of substitution in the ablative and ritualistic exercises that characterized the transition from colonial, rural to urban contexts. Emphasizes a measure of implicating to the symbolic power that subjects the community's agency or jurisdiction as passive. The discourse of acknowledgements and distinctions purports that in the context of substitutions in the ablative exercises, the individual jurisdiction became imbued with an 'initio' or a personal agency related to the epistemic and didactic strategies disseminated by the symbolic power.

The notion of hysteridence seeks to demonstrate that this jurisdiction has a history in the ablative exercises during the substitutions. Where in the arena of cultural identities for example 'signs' became influenced by what is accrued and epistemic. The ablative exercises were contingent on the primordial image of the 'other' and the 'self' in order to establish the jurisdiction of the 'self', 'other' and the jurisdiction of the symbolic power. This way the 'being' can relate the 'self' through instinct or the 'newly' discovered agency. Performance art interrogates this existential space of 'being', in that it seeks to demonstrate that the perception that it is 'pure' or essentialist can only be related to the 'absence' that relates it to the supplement. The primordial image of identity for example instigates the Lacanian triad of the self, symbolic subject and 'other', where the jurisdiction of 'being' as pure can only be related to the didactic facility of the symbolic power.

Performance art is also the arena in which the individual and the community can demonstrate the creativity that is inherent in the passive location in relation to the symbolic power. In the context of the individual in relation to the symbolic power he or she has to be informed by the structure of the unconscious where the essentialist structure of 'signs' is imbued with didactic connotations. In relation to the feminine or contained structure of the symbolic power, where order auto-references and germinates, in the context of the community and performance art, this order operates in a reverse sense or creative sense that characterizes a masculine operation or manifestation. Hill (1992) states that archetypes inform an order that concretizes instinctive operations in 'being', "Even the ideas that the 'artist' or 'genius' has about what is happening to him and what he is doing are archetype conditioned by these perceptions and substructures" (41-42).

The performance artist relies on the structure of the archetype as a resource for creativity and 'representation' where the unconscious can be a source for fictitious characters. It epitomizes the Jungian notion that it is "the instinct's perception of itself"(Hill; 1992, 41), where the notion that the 'self' or 'being' cannot be characterized by essentialist or pure structures as is purported in the context of modernity and in the context of the performance.

Performance art in the context of the 20th century emerged as a necessity to demonstrate the distance between the community and the symbolic power. In that even though the structure and order that the symbolic power imposes has moral implications, the manner in which it disseminates its metaphysical didactic strategies, their connotations can be detected to be imbued with auto-referential connotations. That even though the manner in which it auto-differentiates concretizes its structure and the epistemic location of the community as exalted and passive hysteridentically, it tends to pronounce the operation of 'absence' in the structure of a 'sign' where it becomes possible for a context to exhaust itself.

After the context of social and political upheaval, the order and structure of the symbolic power becomes pronounced for its germinating and distant operation from the community. Performance art on the other hand exposes the opposite function, where it becomes significant for the organic and originary unity that characterizes these relationships to be evident or manifest. This can be demonstrated by the measure with which social and artistic movements like Dadaism emerge in order to demonstrate the supplementary and originary creativity that manifests in the location of the community. Hill (1992) demonstrates how this manifestation is organically ordered and structured due to the organic formative strategies that emerged in relation to the symbolic power. He states that the masculine manifestation or the "....notion of creativity....(comes) empirically from felt experience, live events in actual lives, as psychic perceptions of instinctual processes" (1992: 41).

The measure with which the community is able to express itself can be characterized as the manifestation of the masculine or creativity that emanates and is justified by its referral relationship the symbolic power and the measure with which the community implicates towards the symbolic power. The necessity for order in a social context beset by political upheaval is a result of the originary creativity of the collective when the symbolic power has relinquished its role as the primary didactic facility. This is a context in which the phenomenological experience of the community can be demonstrated to have been influenced by a trace as subjected by the symbolic power and its relationship with 'signs'. In that the collective identity of the collective subsumes both the negative and the positive aspects that the symbolic power deems to characterize its didactic implications.

The discourse of acknowledgments and distinctions seeks to demonstrate that both the negative and the positive aspects of the symbolic power inform the collective diverse identity of the community. Through not just the strategies of implication, but the community has to develop formative strategies that justify and cater for the negative aspect since it is the primary didactic facility. It acknowledges that it is informed by the 'absence' in the structure of the 'sign', it is also that which imbues the negative aspect in the structure of the symbolic power as that which operates as more than just germination facility and propensity. That the order that characterizes the symbolic power is also characterized by a historic trace that is immediate to the cultural and social contexts before the substitution.

Performance art can operate as a social facility that exhibits the measure with which the creativity that manifests in the community is informed by what is hysteridentical in order to demonstrate implicating towards the symbolic power. That the exhaustion that is implicit in the structure of 'signs' in the context of the symbolic power only has relevance for the manner in which it has a relationship with 'signs'. Where the symbolic power is imbued with the facility to exhaust the manner in which it defers to 'signs', and since the community is characterized by an 'absence' in the manner in which it is purported to be related to the symbolic power.

Hysteridence is a notion that seeks to demonstrate that this relationship cannot be exhausted, since the collective is contingent on the symbolic power to concretize its epistemic relationship with the primary didactic facility in the context of the substitution. In that the negative or 'absence' aspect is a facility with which the community can demonstrate it defers to the symbolic power and to purport that this aspect can be exhausted is to render the feminine aspect barren of epistemic logic that imbues it with logocentric certainty. Even though the symbolic power can still be able to defer to itself even when it has 'exhausted' its relationship with the collective it still hast to provide the manner it has a relationship with the epistemic logocentric logic.

The discourse of acknowledgements and distinctions seeks to demonstrate that the feminine principal cannot be exhausted, in the sense that since it accounts for the pre-social processes both of cultural and individual formation that characterize both communities in the rural and urban contexts. In that being cognizant of its 'presence' or 'absence' pre supposes an order that the 'being' and the institutions he or she represents are informed by. Not only do the germination processes demonstrate the measure with which the subjectivity it subsumes to be symbolic when it is imbued a relationship with the supplement. Its supplementary operation becomes imbued with teleological connotations that espouse what is spectral about 'being' in relation to the supplement and what is metaphysical about the symbolic power.

The facility that the archetype affords the performance artist is contingent on the condensation facility in relation to the symbolic power. In that the symbolic power becomes exposed for its epistemic connotations, where its power is both supplementary and operates as a supplement. The archetype also demonstrates the measure with which the metaphysical operation of the symbolic power is contingent on the pre social or originary didactic facility that the supplement affords in order to purport that it is imbued with order and structure without having to demonstrate that in a context where it is witnessable.

In the context where there is social and cultural upheaval, the social context can be subject to change without the context being purported to be a substitution. In that since in the context of advanced modernity the maternal splitting has already always transpired, in that the community and the symbolic power have a binary relationship. Performance art and the resultant organic creativity that characterizes the community is a manifestation for a desire for the maternal aspect in the form of the symbolic power. Since performance art interrogates the measure with which the symbolic power is contingent on the reciprocity of this epistemic relationship not just to justify its teleological or intrinsic value in the cultural dispensation, it also has to demonstrate the measure with which it is a manifestation of creativity.

The facility of the archetype for the individual artist is another manifestation of the symbiotic relationship between the community and the symbolic power. In that both are contingent on the structure of 'signs' as both 'absent' and 'present' facilities. The structure of the archetype in the context of the symbolic power operates with the logocentric logic of essentialism as a mechanism that auto-references to the symbolic power and to the community. In the context of the community and the individual, the archetype is a formative facility imbued with the ambiguity between essentialism and eclectic accretion in the social immediate context. Where it has overt formative implications when it operates with the essentialism it is structured by in the subconscious. It is also that which operates with the implicit collective deferral where it articulates the measure of the inherent psychosis for language and the desire to return for the safety of the maternal figure.

Performance art also articulates the organic order within the immediate social contexts in the cultural dispensation, that since it can utilize the unconscious to demonstrates the measure with which it implicates to the symbolic power, it forces the individual to confront his or her subjectivity in relation to the germinating structure of the symbolic power.

Since the individual is conscious that he or she has 'split' from the symbolic power after the pragmatic and metaphysical operations in the ablative exercises of the substitution, performance art demonstrates the symbolic operation that manifest in the community.

In the context in which Dadaism emerged the creativity that ensued was not only rendered by art practice, but it was imbued with a social aspect that pronounced the 'negative' or 'absence' in the structure of 'signs' in relation to the symbolic power. Where the subjectivity of the community was characterized by operating with the paradigm of being separate from the feminine or containing principle of the symbolic power.

Chapter 7

The 'sign' and the SOCIAL Apparatus

The discourse in this chapter seeks to demonstrate the measure with which the 'sign' is a facility that enables 'being' to be conscious of the manner in which he or she implicates towards the symbolic power. Since the 'sign' operates with a measure of 'absence' in its structure, the discourse will demonstrate how this is how 'being' is induced to implicate towards the symbolic power.

The discourse in this chapter will seek to demonstrate the structure of the 'signifier' or 'meaning' in the context of modernity. It will seek to demonstrate how 'being' or the ontological are that which are crucial in order for 'being' to be conscious of the merger in the context of the substitution from the rural context.

The chapter will also discourse the measure with which the 'sign' instigates conception of 'presence' through the cultural formulation. By demonstrating that the supplement cannot conceive of itself, how the 'sign' or tool is able to instigate conceptions of signification through repetition and ontological repletion.

By demonstrating the significance of being conscious of the symbolic and utilitarian connotations of the 'sign', is what concretizes signification through its inherent facility for deferral. The discourse also seeks to demonstrate the measure with which 'presence' of a tool enables it to be malleable or transformational. When it is related to the 'absence' in the structure of the 'sign', enables 'absence' to be concretized as a condensation facility.

Primarily the chapter seeks to demonstrate the measure with which the 'sign' through accretion and relinquishing characterize a merger between didactic desire and the pragmatic conception of the 'sign'. This way it can demonstrate that the community has its own relationship with the supplement independent of the processes of the symbolic power.

The discourse will also compare the structure of the 'sign' to the structure of the Ich Freud (2003). It will demonstrate the measure with which the Ich is a fragmented microcosm of the 'sign' or tool. It will demonstrate how the 'absence' in the structure of the 'sign' and the ontological space of 'being' are contingent on deferral in order to instigate accretion. That the 'sign' and the ontological space are fragmented in their operation in order to cater for the structure of consciousness in 'being' and to cater for the accretion in the structure of the 'sign' respectively.

The discourse will discourse the teleological or social role of the artist in the context of modernity. This can help detect the significance of 'being' being conscious of the merger with the context after the substitution. How 'being' with his or her psychological drives relates to the symbolic power, does the 'distance' that defines this relationship hinder how 'being' relates to 'signs' and the symbolic power? Does the symbolic power disseminate that the 'absence' in the context of the community is a condensation facility? The discourse will demonstrate that performance art demonstrates the condensation structure of the 'absence' that characterizes this 'absence' characterizes sublimation.

Of the 'sign' and the Social Apparatus

'Meaning' imbues the facility of a 'sign' with a facility for infinite deferral or that which imbues the notion of the didactic with positivist connotations. In the context of archaic man, the 'sign' or tool was a product of accretion in the context of the cultural formulation; the tool or 'sign' did not define the cultural conception, in order to be able to defer. Accretion or 'meaning' has already always been established through desire or what is instinctive about repletion in the ontological context.

Performance art seeks to exhibit that deferral is crucial in the accretion processes of a 'sign', that 'meaning' imbues a 'sign' with form or a measure of structure. That this is contingent upon accretion, repletion and repetition in the ontological and didactic processes of 'being' in an individual context and the deferral that is connoted by desire in a collective and communal context.

The contingency on collective consciousness of performance art seeks to exhibit that agency or the jurisdiction of 'being' is always already symbolic, both in relation to 'being' and in relation to the cultural formulation. The cultural formulation imbues 'being' with deferral or communication facilities, where in order for a 'sign' to operate beyond that which is symbolic in an ontological sense, it has to be constantly be deferred to the 'absence' that necessitates its 'presence' in order to be inculcated in the collective, in order to concretize 'meaning'. Performance art can also exhibit that this constant deferral of the 'sign' is induced by desire or a measure of 'absence' in an ontological sense and that this is a symbolic 'education' through accretion and repetition and repletion.

That 'meaning' is concretized through deferral and repetition, the implement of the spade for example becomes concretized in terms of utilitarian and symbolic connotations. This way 'signs' can be detected for their ambiguous or infinite referral connotations in their structure. Where what is symbolic is accrued through the utilitarian and repetition in the respective arena in which it is utilized in. Where what is symbolic is accrued and concretized through deferral between the particular didactic desire and the particular cultural implement. This way 'meaning' becomes concretized but it also becomes susceptible to deferral, where it is already always cognizant of the fact that accretion and 'presence' or presence are that which render the 'sign' malleable but also to be deferred to the 'absence' of the supplement.

This way it can demonstrate that the 'absence' of the supplement is 'absent' or absent when the implement is imbued with symbolic didactic connotations or it exhibits its metonymic operation. That also it can exhibit that the supplement is 'present' or present through deferral of its temporal operations and the desire in 'being' which can be deferred to what is metaphysical about 'meaning' of the 'sign' or implement.

The 'absence' in the context of modernity with its didactic implications the community and the symbolic power are cognizant of, or 'present' or present. It is symbolic of the operation of the substitution within social choreography. The 'absence' of the didactic can be characterized as a metaphysical inconsistency in the structure of the symbolic power. In that in the context of archaic man, 'absence' was that which induced the metonymic operation of the 'sign' or what was accrued of the cultural formulations and 'signs'. This way the relationship between the cultural conception and the supplement can be imbued with metaphysical connotations when the supplement 'signifies' or justifies not just its own 'presence' or presence, and the presence of 'being' and 'signs'. It can be imbued with pragmatic connotations and implications when the supplement 'signifies' as a didactic facility and the cultural formulation defers to the supplement as the fullest measure of presence in relation to the particular didactic issue.

In the context of modernity it is the symbolic power that this didactic 'absence' defers towards. It is also that which through the
veneration of presence or 'presence' that which renders this 'absence' ontological. In that 'being' is already always imbued with an
'absence' that has didactic relevance to an 'other', the
cultural originary formulations and the structure of the supplement. In the social context this 'absence' becomes pronounced
through the 'presence' and presence of the didactic in the jurisdiction of the 'initio' through the traditional social training. It also
becomes pronounced when the 'absence' in the structure of the
symbolic   power   becomes   apparent   through   the originary jurisdiction in an ontological measure in 'being'.

In the context of the symbolic power, this 'absence' has connotations for accretion and relinquishing in the context of the substitution, where, when and what was concretized was the metaphoric or
condensation structure of 'signs' from the previous cultural paradigm. This way they can still defer, but the measure of deferral is
always towards that which is not 'present' or is informed by the
condensation structure and its static implications.

In that in the unconscious, the condensation structure of a 'sign'
becomes symbolic through what is didactic and is able to 'signify' a
measure of what is didactic in its relationship with the supplement.
Where it becomes concretized as a 'facet' or 'portion' of the supplement. This operation in the 'sign' is also that which constitutes
what is supplementary or the 'signifier' within its structure, where it
is   not   an   internal   opposition,   but   it   can   exhibit   that
to concretize the condensation facility a measure of displacement
has to be 'signified' through an 'absence' in the 'sign'. That form or
what is metaphoric is concretized by an 'absence' that is outside
itself, this way it can auto-reference and when it defers it can exhibit
that accretion is significant in the concretization of its form.

Form and presence/'presence' in the context of modernity are
that which are attributed with positivist connotations, they are also
that which are consistent with 'signification' as both a positivist
facility and a metaphoric facility. In that a metaphoric facility imbues the facility of the 'initio' with epistemic and accretion implications, the metaphoric facility is also that which imbues the measure
of the 'absence' as that which is imbued with metaphysical
connotations.

When a 'sign' is imbued with metaphysical connotations it can be
deduced to be comprised of form, and form is the indication that

what is epistemic has influenced its measure of accretion and relinquishing. That which is imbued with a measure of the metaphysical operates as condensation or metaphoric facility. In the context of modernity's cultural paradigm the metaphoric facility is imbued with an 'authority' or a jurisdiction that concretizes the formative in relation to the supplement. That it is concretized by the deferral towards the supplement in a measure that is about what is symbolic of the measure of the didactic lesson accounting for a portion of the fullest measure of presence.

In the context of the substitution from the rural to the urban context, in order to concretize what is epistemic and related to the supplement in the structure of the 'sign', and in order to account for the 'absence' with its didactic implications. The symbolic power conceived of the condensation facility as fixed in order to account in a positivist and practical measure for the 'absence' of didactic encounters between diverse cultures and communities. This 'absence' also allows 'signs' to differentiate themselves from themselves in a measure that accounts for the didactic paradigm in the context of the substitution and the ontological existential location of 'being'. It also allows the notion of the collective community to be clustered into a singularity that is different from the singularity of the supplement, the supplement which has maintained its metaphysical and didactic connotations even in the context of the substitution.

The measure of 'absence' and its didactic connotations in the context of the substitution or modernity is barren of the formative and the metaphysical. That the infinite deferral that is connoted by art practice in deferral or in relation to the symbolic power, can demonstrate that the symbolic power is a 'representer' or a usurper of the conscious ontological space. That it achieves this through the facility of the 'initio' that is inculcated as accounting for the 'absence' in the diverse context of the substitution that modernity can exhibit through deferral to the epistemic and historic operation of the 'sign'.

The significance of art practice seeks to exhibit that in the context of modernity the jurisdiction of agency cannot be 'barren' of didactic implications. In that if there is an 'absence' in the cultural dispensation, then there is already always a measure of the metaphysical that is operational within the community and in the structure of 'signs'. This can be detected in the operation of the 'initio', that since its 'production' emanates from the structure of the initium or the enunciative field of communication and deferral, then the measure of 'absence' is informed by the epistemic and that which is metaphoric of the 'absence' of the supplement.

Art practice can exhibit that this 'absence' is already always an operational aspect or a supplementary aspect of the substitution and the symbolic power. In that that 'absence' of the supplement enables 'signs' to be imbued with future implications or the transformational propensities of the metonymic propensity.

If the assumption that 'being' is an auto-referential entity then in order to operate as an auto-referential entity this measure of 'absence' that characterizes the context of modernity should account for the fullest measure of presence or the 'emptiness' that the symbolic power purports diverse encounters are connoted by. This way the operation of the 'sign' is always that which is subject to that which is to come, but if in the context of this 'absence' the measure of that which is to come is contingent on the pre-reflective that the traditional social training and the 'initio' purport. Not only is the context barren of a juxtaposition facility but it is also barren of the measure for 'being' to imbue the metaphorical operation of the 'sign' with the necessary transformational or metonymic operations. This way the measure that enables 'being' to be an internal adequation with oneself can be related to the supplement in order for the social moment to not 'exhaust' itself within the 'moment' but also to enable accretion in relation to an epistemic operation of the 'sign'. If the 'sign' or 'being' operates with this pre-reflective measure, art practice can demonstrate that this still enables 'being' to be imbued with the measure of the jurisdiction that is about desire for the didactic. If it is about the pre-reflective then it can still be related or deferred to a relationship with the supplement, unlike the 'absence' in the context of modernity.

In the auto-referential context of performance art for example, the immediacy that the context is informed by is structured in the measure of the exhausted social context according to the traditional training. But it exhibits that 'being' is that whose originary agency is susceptible to auto-differentiation and differentiation unlike the indivisibility that is connoted by the 'initio' according to traditional social training. In that the auto-differentiation that is connoted in the context of performance art t is comprised of the implications of the future, where the 'moment' is illuminated by accretion and the metonymic operation of 'signs'. That the exhaustion of the moment and its implications for the future are the measure with which 'being' concretizes condensation facilities as orientation facilities that imbue the emptiness' or 'absence' of the supplement with a discourse of fullest measure of presence.

Performance art can deduce that the facility of the fullest measure of presence, or the supplement enables 'being' to extend the subject beyond the ontological and into collective, by exhibiting that 'signs' have a relationship with contexts, prior, during and after the 'moment'. The measure with which 'being' is able to extend beyond the 'moment' is through the differentiation facility that the symbolic subject in the cerebral spaces of 'being', and renders the symbolic space of 'being' as metaphoric. It is also that which enables deferral to that which is the symbolic subject to be transformational.

In the context of the performance art, the measure with what is 'play' is able to be imbued with didactic or formative discourse seeks to exhibit that 'being' is imbued with an originary agency. This agency concretizes the location of the supplement as 'empty' in that in order for this emptiness to defer it has to encounter the desire in 'being' for that which is didactic or related to the cultivation of knowledge or the epistemic.

Since the cultural formulation can exhibit that 'being' cannot account for the plenitude connoted by the 'emptiness' it accounts for the 'presence' and presence of 'being' that in the context of the cultural formulation is symbolic of a portion of the plenitude or the fullest measure of presence.

When the discourse attributes portions to the fullest measure of presence it is due to the ontological and existential measure in the conception of the didactic formulation in relation to the supplement. In that in order for the didactic to operate as a supplementary, 'being' has to conceive of it through the processes of accretion and repetition that can exhibit that the supplement is a deferral facility and symbolic of the plenitude that is connoted by the 'emptiness' of the supplement.

In the context of modernity the measure with which 'being' is able to maintain agency is through this 'absence', it is significant for 'being' to be imbued with a measure of agency in order to concretize the cultural formulation as a condensation or metaphoric facility. In the context of modernity this measure of 'absence' can exhibit that the ontological desires what is didactic, the measure that has concretized the binary and imbued it with metaphysical connotations between the community and the symbolic power. That this can be characterized to be contingent on the metaphysical presence and 'presence' of the originary cultural formulations.

That when the discourse states that the symbolic power or the cultural formulations are that which are symbolic of a portion of the fullest measure of presence they are that which are contingent on the presence or 'presence' of the originary cultural formulations in order to concretize the measure with which the symbolic power in the context of modernity has formulated the binary relationship between the community and itself.

In the context of performance art presence and 'presence' operate with metaphysical connotations in that 'being' is able to differentiate in the Lacanian structure of the conscious. He or she is able to occupy the location of the symbolic subject, where the facility of the 'initio' can be cultivated in the context of the traditional social training and the 'being' can auto-differentiate in the context of the performance art.

This is the grounds upon which the discourse can characterize 'being' as a social apparatus, in that not only is 'being' symbolic of the symbolic power, but 'being' is also evidence of its 'presence' or its presence through the facility of the 'initio' and the implication to the symbolic power. The notion of an apparatus requires the subject or object of the discourse to be witnessable in a palpable measure. The discourse has sought to determined that what is palpable is also able to defer and be imbued with metaphysical connotations as in the measure of the 'object' as that which is able to auto-reference and defer to the supplement.

The measure with which an apparatus is contingent on that which is metaphysical is that it must concretize the desired notion as that which is auto-referential in the cerebral spaces of 'being' and it can defer to the supplement. It must 'differentiate' itself in relation to itself, but it must also operate as a differentiation facility for 'being' in relation to the cultural formulation, as both evidence of the 'presence' of the cultural formulation and presence of the supplement.

The symbolic power requires an apparatus in order to account for the 'absence' of didactic strategies in the oeuvre of the unconscious and the conscious. This can be detected in the operation of the initium or the enunciative field in the organic or originary social transactions prior and during the advent of the substitution into the context of modernity. In the enunciative field, it is not 'being' who is in competition, rather the 'signs' are that which are in competition, that this can be detected in their oscillation between metonymic and metaphoric operations, where in relation to an 'other' and to that which is supplementary the 'sign' assumes metonymic operations and when the 'sign' defers to the supplement or what is didactic in the cultural formulation, operates as a metaphoric facility.

The 'sign', 'meaning' and hysteridence

The 'sign' in the context of the cultural formulation seeks to demonstrate the 'presence' of the supplement. 'Being' in this context is imbued with the facility of deferral, but this deferral 'being' has to be cognizant of as the symbolic subject in relation to an external source or subject or reference, that comprises what is intuitive and originary about desire. In the social context the propensity for deferral has to operate in the cognitive through temporal deferral or social intercourse. The location that 'being' occupies is symbolic to the extent that the thing that is desired is 'absent' or has relevance to the supplement in a metaphysical manner, where order and deferral enable auto-references propensity to the supplement. 'Meaning' is the facility with which the 'sign' becomes concretized as the symbolic subject in the Lacanian structure of the psyche, then it can be deduced that it renders 'being' symbolic in relation to the cultural formulation and in relation to the community. To demonstrate how 'meaning' enables sublimation in the structure of the psyche we examine how Freud identified the Ich in the structure of the psyche and he describes it in the following manner.

"It also fulfills its task with respect to the inner world, that is, with respect to the Es, by gaining mastery over the demands of the drives, by deciding whether they should be allowed gratification, by postponing this gratification, until the time and circumstances are favorable in the external world, or by suppressing their excitations altogether. Its actions directed by observing the tensions that are either already present in it or have been introduced into it" (Freud; 2003, 176-177. "An Outline of Psychoanalyses").

In the context of performance art the 'being' or the cognitive substance that can be designated as the Ich is a facility with which 'being' auto-references, is able to differentiate him or herself from self. It is a facility where 'meaning' assumes symbolic implications and intellectual illumination. Its structures can be deduced to also be characterized by the ambiguity of auto-referencing, in that the 'being' is conscious of the ambiguity of an external source and its internal implications for desire.

In the context of performance art, the 'being' has access to this facility of 'meaning' as an auto-differentiation facility, where its supplementary implications have social and cultural connotations. Then he or she is able to utilize the deferral propensity of the 'sign' through its accretion with historic and epistemic implications. In order to demonstrate the extent to which he or she has reconciled his or her implication to the symbolic power, or the extent to which he or she is a social 'being'. In that to reconcile is to demonstrate one's comprehension of the 'absence' that characterizes the submissive location that occupies that location in the relationship with symbolic power. As Freud has sought to demonstrates:

> *"the Ich has control over voluntary movement. It has the task of self-assertion, and fulfills it with respect to the 'outside' world by getting to know the stimuli there, by storing information about them (in the memory), by avoiding excessively strong stimuli (through flight), by dealing with moderate stimuli (through adaptation) and finally by learning to change the external world in an expedient way to its own language (through activity)" (pp. 176-177)*

To describe the Ich as the facility for sublimation, where the 'being' establishes 'being' as symbolic in relation to self and the external world is apt. This is consistent with the ethic of social consciousness that performance art overtly discourses, in that not only does 'being' as a symbolic entity desire a didactic facility that has a relationship with the supplement, it is also the facility with which 'being' questions the discourse of the current social dispensation. It achieves this through the fragmentation that characterizes 'being', the social context and its implications for orientation and external stimuli, and the exchange 'being' instigates with the symbolic power through implication.

This was also characterized by the role that Dadaism played in the global cultural dispensation in the wake of the war that erupted during the years that it was flourishing as creative social critique discourse. Traditional ethics based on violence regarding the manner in which global conflicts can be solved became sublimated in various aspect of the society but not those of the symbolic power.

In the context of performance art, the notion of sublimation becomes immediate to the relationship the 'being' has implicated with the symbolic power. In that not only does it question the discourse of negativity and the didactic facility that institutes an 'absence' in the structure of the 'sign' that characterizes the passive location of the community and 'being'. It is also a strategy to interrogate the status quo in the cultural dispensation, in that even if performance art gained prominence after movements like Dadaism, the propensity and significance for deferral in the practice, demonstrated that deferral has connotations for the epistemic and the contemporary simultaneously. This way the propensity for infinite referral in the structure of the 'sign' has immediate connotations for repetition and repletion.

The performance artist then is cognizant of the measure with which he or she has implications for sublimation and transformation both in his or her immediate relationship with the 'sign', than with the negative condensation aspect formulated by the symbolic power. The artist eschews the one-dimensional aspect of the symbolic power with its implications for 'absence', rather the artist assumes a didactic conception based on creativity in order to be able to differentiate self from self, in order to differentiate the cultural formulation from the supplementary, and the supplementary from the supplement.

What is metaphysical in the arena of performance art and art practice in general is imbued with the powers of the artist perception, that which in psychoanalysis Jung designates as the artist "rising above the personal and speaking from the mind and heart of the artist to the mind and heart of man" (1966; 101). What is metaphysical is also related to the measure with which what is supplementary can be detected to be imbued with the propensity for sublimation that is about the originary creativity in the formulation of a culture, taking into consideration the concretization of aesthetics,

the realization of the didactic informative strategies and their propensities for external influence and so forth.

Performance art then operates with this character of "participation mystique...that is the secret of artistic creation and the effect
which great art has upon us, for at that level of experience it is no
longer the weal or woe of the individual that counts, but the life of
the collective" (1966; 105). Consistent with the operation of the Ich,
the artist can immerse oneself into the discourse he or she is interrogating, with the facility of utilizing and engaging of physical
drives and unconscious drives.

In the context of advanced modernity, the condensation operations of the symbolic power hinder drives both as implicating tools
and social interaction capabilities as that which are barren of
the originary didactic facility to orientate 'being' in the context of
the community. Since the condensation structure in the binary
location in the relationship with the symbolic power in the context
of the community is characterized by an 'absence', performance art
is able to demonstrate the measure with which this condensation
strategy is also susceptible to sublimation in the cognitive space of
'being'. Since the condensation facility of 'absence' or negativity
can be transformed by the very structure that disseminates it, the
artist is able to immerse oneself into the ambiguous drama between
the significant presence/'presence' of the symbolic power and its
epistemic
discourse.

What is hysteridentical according to the discourse of acknowledgements and distinctions is that the condensation facility of
'absence' and negativity in the context of the community is comprised of the same structure of deferral as the condensation facility
of 'presence' and positivity in the context of the symbolic power. In
that the 'absence'/absence in the context of the community as a
condensation facility has the same epistemic source as the 'presence'/presence of the symbolic power. They were both subject and
are products of the same sublimation connotations and implications in the context of the ablative exercises that characterized the
historic and epistemic substitutions of colonial and postcolonial
contexts.

Chapter 8

Condensation or Metaphoric Location of Submission and Art Practice

The discourse in this chapter will examine how 'being' in the context of modernity is conscious of his or her submissive location in the relationship with the symbolic power. How in the Black Consciousness movement artists and their resistance art produced work that not only characterized a cultural category, they also demonstrated the deconstructionist notion of auto-negation that 'being' is subject to in the context of modernity.

In this chapter the discourse has to demonstrate the measure with which 'signs' in the social context are exhaustible. The discourse will demonstrate how the 'sign' can be concretized as 'pure' or 'essentialist'.

It will also demonstrate how resistance art in South African spread consciousness through the cultural dispensation about the essentialist operation of the 'sign'.

By citing Hegarty (2004) who explicates Buadrillard's understating of consumer ethics in the context of modernity, the discourse will demonstrate how what is hysteridentical is defined by the blurred lines between consumers from low income and high-income communities being informed by the same consumer ethics. That this essentialist structure not only has relevance in consumer ethics, but in the context of resistance art in South Africa concretized the measure with which political 'signs' were imbued with the logic of logocentrism.

The discourse will demonstrate how resistance art (http://www.contemporary-african-art.com/resistance-art.htm) can demonstrate the nature of auto-negation in the context of modernity, that its essential 'sign' can be detected to be that which has connotations for rendering the submissive location a condensation. The chapter will demonstrate how the art movement discoursed social, cultural and political issues. The Black Consciousness Movement in South Africa inspired art by artists like Penny Siopsis, Gavin Janties, Willie Bester, Sue Williamson and Helen Sibidi.

For the discourse of acknowledgments and distinctions it is significant to demonstrate the measure with which the social context is structured in terms of signification. This way it can discourse the measure with which 'signs' in the social context defer towards the fullest measure of presence or the supplement without accounting for it.

In that the discourse seeks to demonstrate how it is significant for the symbolic power that the community as well does not account for the fullest of presence, where and when deferring or establishing a relationship with the supplement. In Mbembe's discourse this deferral is articulated as that which is relevant for strategies of signification in a particular epoch. In the context of modernity strategies of deferral emanate from there being a "close relationship between subjectivity and temporality" (2001:14). The discourse will demonstrate how signification in the context or period that resistance art thrived in South Africa operated in an hysteridentical measure. Through being conscious of the measure with which 'signs' are influenced by organic processes in the community and formulated in the processes of the symbolic power.

Through art and the symbolic implication of consumerism, and the ambiguous structure in the relative or hysteridentical connotations between low income and high consumers, the structure of signification can be detected to be necessary in order to establish a relationship with the supplement.

The discourse will also seek to demonstrate how this signification can be detected in the organic facility of the symbolic power, where it can be detected that both the community and the symbolic power rely on to establish a relationship with 'signs'.

Of condensation locations and art

Being' can be characterized as an apparatus in the context of modernity in that he or she occupies the location in the community where he is metaphoric of submission and anarchy. The significance of the condensation facility is that it provides the cultural formulation with a comprehension of a portion of the fullest measure of presence. That it is the 'sign' being concretized as imbued with form, but also the ambiguity of presence and absence in its structure. As both that which is about deferral to what is temporal and what is metaphysical. Submission and anarchism are that which are temporal manifestations, they become accrued in the initium or the enunciative field, they are also part of the didactic and formative manifestations or examples of how 'being' desire what is didactic even at a collective conscious level.

It is context that determines what 'presence' or presence is operational in the 'sign', in the sense that in the binary structure, the 'initio' is imbued with power or superiority when there is a 'being' who is 'barren' of the didactic training that informs this power. At the instant of operation, the 'sign' has to be cognizant of a measure of 'absence', both within its structure and the immediate 'absence' outside its form. These not only pronounce that 'presence' is operational in the 'sign', they also concretize the binary notion to be imbued with a measure of the metaphysical that exhibits that the 'sign' or 'being' is cognizant of the logic of logocentrism in the structure of the symbolic power. The presence that 'being' and the 'sign' are cognizant of, is inculcated as the essentialist aspect in the operation of the 'sign'.

Art practice has sought to exhibit that this operation in the context of modernity not only renders the 'sign' as an apparatus, it is also that which through the 'presence' enables 'being' to reveal the secret of auto-negation or self implicating to the symbolic power.

The artist reveals implicating through his practice for example and the city official through the power imbedded in his jurisdiction. Resistance artists like Willie Bester through his piece "Forced removal" (1988) discourses the aspect of origins in the context modernity. Through the piece the essentialist notion of communities through political, racial and economic connotations the artist demonstrate the measure with which communities subject to forced removals were concretized with condensation of being poor or peripheral in relation to the city center. It became easy to dichotomize them with the urban city center for example.

Another piece that demonstrates in a symbolic manner the measure with which the 'essential' 'sign' in modernity is symbolic is Manfred Zylla's "Death Trap" (1985) which is a piece that discourse of the Trojan Horse episode (http://www.sahistory.org.za/dated-event/trojan-horse-massacre) in the township of Athlone in 1985, where police shot and killed anti-apartheid protesters.

The piece is a pencil on paper rendition, with a police van crammed with police and a photograph on a dark patch on the ground. The solitary photograph on the ground is symbolic of the distance between the community and the symbolic power. The police are not only symbolic of the violence that the apparatus provides the symbolic power, they also operate as an essentializing border between the community and the symbolic power.

These art works demonstrated the measure with which 'signs' in the historical context of modernity as Mbembe (2001) demonstrates in his discourse of the notion of the postcolony, structures of signification become diffused through repetition and are contingent on the provisional facility of the symbolic power that through art practice can demonstrate has 'alternative' didactic goals from the community. What is hysteridentical emerges and becomes concretized when "distinctive and particular things are constituted by a set of material practices, signs, figures, superstitions, images, and fictions that, because they are available to individual's imagination and intelligence and actually experienced, form what might be called "language of life" (2001:15). What he means by material practices and 'language of life' are the socially organic formative strategies in the context of the community that are imbued with existential connotations. They are informed by this 'absence' in the metaphoric and condensation structure of 'signs' in the context of the community and are imbued with existential creativity and influenced by the structure of signification that concretize the binary of dominance and passivity between the community and symbolic power.

The discourse of acknowledgements and distinctions can demonstrate that what is hysteridentical can also be characterized as that which Mbembe deems of the 'language of life'. In that since what is hysteridentical is determined by a measure of what is 'negative' and 'positive', low culture and high culture, both discourses demonstrate their contingency on 'signs' being informed by the same organic and formulated structures. Both discourses emphasize the existential creativity that cannot be avoided and is necessary for orientation purposes.

Therefore it becomes significant to reveal the secret of implication. In that part of revealing the secret, is to self differentiate, but it is also the measure with which 'being' exhibits his or her will to desire what is didactic, and that the symbolic power, utilizes the measure in 'being' where to desire for the didactic is constantly a facility for deferral. That to desire is such a constant that it can be attributed to the essentialism that concretizes the 'sign' as that which is 'pure' and imbued only with the characteristics of 'presence' or presence.

Since there is an 'absence' of didactic strategies in the context of the substitution, it becomes pragmatic for the symbolic power to purport that the community and 'being' desire what is formative and didactic that can be witnessed to be informed by universal connotations and implications. In that the social transaction can be witnessed is barren of didactic strategies in the witnessable form of the 'being' who is barren of the facility of the 'initio'.

The symbolic power is cognizant of the accretion and epistemic fact that submission and what is anarchistic are that which are provided and accommodated in the context of the unconscious also with metaphoric and condensation implications. This can be detected in the passive and submissive role that the 'other' in the colonial encounter was imbued with. That 'othering' operated with between cultural groups as a result of the proverbial anti-thesis locations that an 'other' and his or her culture occupy in the respective initium or enunciative field of a particular cultural epoch.

In the pre-colonial context, the 'other' was that which occupied an ambiguous or ambivalent location between desire for the new knowledge he or she had to represent the structures of knowledge in the rural context. The operation of the initium can be characterized as the semiotic operation of 'signifiers' and 'signs' in a particular context, that in the context of the substitution, the rural context became concretized and articulated as an anti-thesis to the didactic conception in the structure of modernity.

The symbolic power has been exhibited is contingent on the semiotic drives of the context prior the establishment of modernity, through the epistemic informing the essentialism of the binary or dichotomy structure of the 'sign'. In the context of archaic man, the value of temporal deferral was that it imbued the 'sign' with positivist connotations that rendered the facility of repetition through both practice and deferral in the cerebral spaces of 'being' as that which is metaphysical but also as that which imbues 'being' with the jurisdiction of agency that is originary and ontological.

Semiotic drive or accretion of 'meaning' in the structure of a 'sign' can be imbued with metaphoric connotations, that even when the 'sign' is informed by negative structures, it will be concretized in the structure of the conscious and unconscious as that which is negative. In order for a negative 'sign' to be concretized as such, it has to be able to defer to both 'signs' and 'signifiers' it is consistent with in terms of operation and 'signs' that are oppositional to it in the same manner. When in the deconstructionist discourse it is stated that 'signs' are essentialist when they are dissimulating themselves, concretized not just as form, but also concretized the temporal deferral measure in the cerebral connotations of 'being' as will, or semiotic drive or the concretization of the jurisdiction of agency. They are that which concretize the logic of the cultural formulation as a didactic facility that has relevance for presence/'presence' of what is supplementary.

And when Kristeva states that 'signs' can loose a measure of re-presentation in their structure, is that they have to concretize the measure of their own auto-reference, or their own auto-partition. This was part of the semiotic operation in the colonial encounter between cultures from different parts of the world and their respective relationship with the fullest measure of presence in the context of the substitutions. When the deconstructionist discourse purports that 'signs' dissimulate their 'meaning', this is the measure with which the 'sign' imparts and concretizes its jurisdiction.

In the context of modernity, this dissimulation has had to be imbued with a measure of 'deception' that is about concretizing power in 'being' and concertizing communal ethics that this discourse characterizes as hysteridentical. In that since the community is distant from the symbolic power and contingent on it for didactic implications that are supplementary. This 'deception' becomes the sole means with which the symbolic power becomes concretized as logocentric and epistemic.

Hysteridence is a product of the semiotic drive or force at the heart of modernity that concretizes the jurisdiction of power or agency to be imbued with essentialist connotations. Since the 'sign' is imbued with essentialist structures, it in the context of the community precipitates desire for the didactic. Since 'being' and the community occupy symbolic locations in relation to the symbolic power it can be detected that the structure of the 'sign' is also a product of the deferral of the didactic 'signifiers' in the structure of the symbolic power.

In the social context, the 'sign' has to concretize itself through the 'absence' that is immediate to itself, or as Kristeva states 'signs' can also concretize that which is 'unrepresentable' in the structure of the 'signifier', where it 'creates' its own partition. In the context of modernity, where the facility of the 'initio' is the primary orientation and didactic facility, that which cannot be represented in the structure of this 'sign' is passive, submissive or anarchistic in the symbolic location of the community or the 'being'. Since the social transaction is subject to repetition, the 'being' who is barren of the 'initio', becomes subject to metaphoric or condensation structures as didactic discourse in a measure that seeks to demonstrate that the 'initio' is a positive logical didactic facility, that dissimulates or 'deceives' through negative deferral in order to exhibit an 'other' is 'unrepresentable' within the structure of the 'initio' and the symbolic power.

It is the essentialism in the structure of the 'initio' whose semiotic measure is also imbued with essentialist connotations that exhibit that the submissive location of the community and 'being' are unrepresentable in the structure of the 'initio'. Since the social transaction is subject to repetition and that the 'initio' cannot appropriate the alternative organic strategies in the context of the community, this is also the measure with which it has to be cognizant of in terms the dissimulation strategy that informs the structure of the 'initio'. The point where the 'sign' becomes cognizant of its auto-reference or auto-negation propensities.

The discourse of acknowledgements and distinctions states that hysteridence is the manifestation in the context of modernity of the aspects in social transactions of that which cannot be appropriated and represented by the primary condensation facility in the structure of the symbolic power and the logic of logocentrism.

Art movements are able to unearth and trace what is hysteri-denctical in the structure of the 'sign' and in the context of the immediate social transaction. In that art movements are able to exhibit the measure with which 'signs' appropriate the ethics and values of the negative and dominant jurisdiction that characterize the metaphoric operation of the didactic facility in the context of modernity. The discourse of acknowledgements and distinctions can exhibit what Kristeva's discourse considers to be 'unrepresentable' in the context of the didactic in the structure of the 'sign'. It is that which the discourse characterizes as the casual ethics and values in the organic transactions between 'being' without the facility of the 'initio' in the social context. What is hysteridentical is characterized by adaptation into the urban context, being cognizant and conscious of the 'absence' that informs the didactic connotations of the relationship between the community and the symbolic power and the resultant auto-affection of being conscious of the ontological and teleological role of the 'initio'. That what cannot be appropriated into the operation of the 'initio' is characterized as submissive or anarchic, even passive, in that not only are these concretized as condensation facilities in the unconscious and certain social contexts, but in the logocentric logic they operate as that which are metaphoric of the submissive location in the essentialist binary conception.

In the context of the court room for example, the perpetrator always occupies a submissive or passive location, in that he or she is concretized in a location where he is defending, either what is his ontological jurisdiction or that which is a product of traditional training and its conceptions of the didactic.

That which is informed by the originary cultural formulation in the context of the community is in the form of property, spiritual inclinations, values of wealth and the acquisition of the wealth, notions about 'otherness' in the context of the initium as deferred from the context prior the substitution into modernity, homogenous narratives in the context of the city and the demographics that are purported to comprise it.

Not only are the characteristics of what is ontological in a particular culture unable to be articulated and appropriated in a measure that 'signs' operate within another culture, but the symbolic power characterizes this universal measure as that which is the 'absence' in the context of the substitution and that was the epistemic foundations for the logic of 'presence' or presence or that which is positivist or witnessable to be primary didactic and orientation facility.

The metaphoric or condensation facility in the context of modernity is iimbued with positivist connotations and implications, in order to provide the community with a didactic facility that concretizes in an existential and ontological measure what it characterizes as a substitution into modernity. In an existential measure the 'absence' becomes incorporated into the arbitrary structure and operation of language and 'signs', this it can be exhibited is informed by what is epistemic and is a product of the proverbial enunciative field or that which this discourse characterizes as the initium.

The submissive and anarchistic location of the binary in the context of the symbolic power is also informed by the language of the unconscious in the sense that it can be traced in the accretion of 'signs' and their didactic measure in the unconscious. For example if one takes the archetype of the trickster in the plethora of 'signs' in the unconscious, not only does it have universal connotations, but it also subsumes most significantly the measure of the originary jurisdiction with its existential and ontological implications. In that the trickster is the archetype where the ambiguity of negativity and positivity informs its semiotic structure.

The 'initio' in the symbolic structure

The facility of the 'initio' on the other hand is informed by the master archetype in the context of modernity. In that not only does 'being' in the context of modernity have to be conscious of diversity as a didactic facility, but he or she has to subsume it to inform and be informed by his or her traditional didactic training in the operations of the symbolic power.

The teleological implications behind the condensation or metaphoric operation of the submissive location in the context of modernity is that it provides the discursive training a facility to concretize the perception of the 'pure' or essentialist 'sign' in the operations of the symbolic power. The symbolic power has inculcated that the context of the substitution was a deferral and accretion process, this can be detected in the necessary didactic implications between 'being' and 'other', but also the dissemination of knowledge and its institutions in the context of modernity. Where didactic implications became concretized with epistemic connotations and were able to eschew the exegetic in the structure of 'signs'.

This not only serves to concretize the 'absence' in the location and 'sign' of the community. But it also serves to concretize that 'being' is imbued with an originary jurisdiction that is 'barren' of the pure and essentialist structure of the 'initio'.

That the didactic implications between 'being' and 'other' in the context of substitution, was imbued and informed by the operation of 'signs' in the context or arena of the initium or the enunciative field. The symbolic power is also informed by the initium in the measure that it provides strategies and facilities that concretize the measure with which 'signs' operate with positivist connotations and concretize the notion of 'presence' or presence as that which informs the 'sign'.

In the context of modernity that which is witnessable in an ontological measure is attributed to the physical manifestation of conscious drives that in the social context becomes concretized through the logic of immediacy and transience. The ambiguity of 'presence' and 'absence' in the context of modernity in the social context becomes imbued with a measure of the didactic in that the physical drives of 'being' cannot be reconciled in the context of symbolic power's traditional training, they are rather imbued with a measure originary agency that has a relationship with the supplement, and concretize the supplementary operation of the submissive location in the logocentric binary as a metaphoric facility.

In that it can be characterized as physical constitutes 'presence', and that the measure with which 'being' defers his or her 'presence' to an 'other' is contingent on the measure of this 'presence' being transient and 'absent' in the strategies of traditional social training. That the notion of the 'pure' 'sign' is related to accretion in a measure that accrues and concretizes the strategy and location of 'absence' as that which when it is ontological becomes associated with what is oppositional to the symbolic power. When it is didactic it is always already in the process of deferral that subsume what is universal and related to both physical drives of 'being' and his or her unconscious. In that both 'being' and 'other' have to acknowledge the 'presence' of the 'being' with the 'initio' or the 'sign' that concretizes the didactic and the symbolic 'presence' or presence of the symbolic power.

That when it is associated with physical drives, it is evidence of presence or 'presence' of the processes of auto-affection, which according to the symbolic power, in order to concretize the objectivity that the facility of the 'initio' subsumes is that the emotional connotations of auto-affection become concretized as the metaphoric or condensation structure of the submissive and anarchistic location in the dichotomous relation between 'being' and the symbolic power.

The discourse is not stating that the submissive location in the binary relationship between 'being' and the symbolic power is 'barren' of a relationship with the supplement, nor is it stating that the symbolic power is inculcating this. Rather, this location can exhibit that since the cultural formulation cannot account for the fullest measure of presence in relation to the supplement, the submissive or 'negative' aspect in the metaphoric vocabulary of the unconscious not only operates as a transformational facility in relation to the internal autonomic operations of 'being'. It is also that which is symbolic of the aspect of the supplement that is indefinite, can be characterized as emptiness, symbolic of an internal ambiguity in the operation of the supplement. That the supplement can be characterized as anachronistic when the supplement operates in a positive sense and informs the particular didactic concern in relation to the fullest measure of presence. That when it is negative it exhibits the measure with which the didactic or the 'negative' force also cannot account for the fullest measure of presence. This not only precipitates the creativity of the cultural formulation, it also concretizes the supplementary operation and location of 'being'.

Therefore the symbolic power is able to exhibit the measure with which auto-affection is out of place in the operations of the didactic implications of the symbolic power. This anachronism extends to the extent of the social context, in the form disregarding the physical drives that inform the epistemic operation of the unconscious and the conscious. The supplement also can attest to the supplementary nature of the 'negative' aspect both in its submissive stance, but also in its combative measure, that they can both be didactic in a measure that is about the supplement being a 'signifier' that is auto-referential through the instigation of the cultural formulation. That the cultural formulation requires the supplement in order to concretize the measure with which how the indivisibility of 'being' under the auspices of modernity also requires a relationship with the supplement. In that this way both aspects of the binary can be detected to be imbued with a relationship with the representational aspect of the cultural formulation, where 'being' and the 'sign' can exhibit their propensity for juxtaposition.

Consumerism as hysteridentical

The discourse of acknowledgement and distinctions has sought to demonstrate that the ablative exercises that characterized the historical contexts of colonization and the institutionalization of advanced modernity where contingent on the epistemic notion of fullest measure of presence in order to account for the diversity that they were confronted with. The exercises were contingent on the symbolic location and operation of 'being' as both an agent of the symbolic power and a passive witness to the substitution that was being instituted.

The discourse also discourses the notion of the 'initio' in the context of 'being' imbued with the jurisdiction, that it is the didactic facility in the formulations of the symbolic power in order to mark beginnings in both historic contexts and in minute social interactions. The 'initio' is evidence of the presence/'presence' of condensation facilities in the cultural dispensation that are imbued with universal connotations and implications. In contrast to the psyche between the artist and city official for example, where the artist can be imbued with metaphysical connotations, the 'initio' or the 'beginnings' of intercourse between 'being' under the symbolic power of officialdom and 'being' in the socially organic context like the artist. The 'initio' can be characterized as the official training and austere conduct, 'presence' and 'absence' become overt facilities of formative training and can be detected to inform the structure of 'signs'.

Baudrillard has demonstrated that these social locations, with their subjective implications towards the epistemic and mutual relationship with the symbolic power, had in the context of modernity come to represent different schools of knowledge and interaction between the institutions that inform formative and socializing strategies. The discourse of acknowledgements and distinctions seeks to demonstrate the measure with which the originary and organic implications of these strands of knowledge in the cultural dispensation has fostered and concretized the binary logic in the relationship between the symbolic power and the community.

Hegarty demonstrates how Baudrillard explicates the impact of this binary. According to the discourse of acknowledgments and distinctions it is that with which can be characterized as hysteridentical. In highlighting the ideological conception of a consumer society Hegarty explicates Baudrillard understanding that;

> *"Consumer society is not, for Baudrillard a 'self-integrating', class differentiated social structure as Gane puts it (Bestiory p.70). Hierarchy does persist, and growth is a function of the system for maintaining its inequities (Consumer, p53,67), but the vital aspect is one of perceived freedom and mobility that arises when all (can) be bought (p61, 79-80) and that differentiation is unli-*

mited" (Hegarty, 2004; 20). "Jean Baudrillard: Live Theory"

It can be deduced from this excerpt that what is hysteridentical requires those that occupy that location in the context of the community to be conscious of the immediate social and cultural implications in the social context. It also demonstrates that it is imperative that they should be conscious of their ambiguous location in relation to knowledge and their location in relation to the didactic conception of the consumer in advanced capitalism.

And those that are imbued with the discursive training that concretizes the hierarchy and the logic of growth to constitute both a strand or quality of knowledge and social hierarchies in the cultural dispensation is a manifestation of the measure with which the binary logic in the culture is contingent on the symbiotic relationship between the community and the symbolic power.

In that the symbolic power is disseminated as a harbinger of 'high culture' since the community is characterized by an 'absence' in terms of being a 'sign' that is imbued with a relationship with 'high culture' from an epistemic perspective. Even though the symbolic power is the facility with which the 'absence' and the 'high culture' are disseminated it occupies the role of also having to cultivate the proper disposition. In that the symbolic power has to be cognizant of the measure with which 'high culture' is also informed by the arbitrary nature of the initium and the stratification of the discursive in its processes.

What is hysteridentical is to recognize the 'distance' from the cultural formulation, but still be able to negotiate it in the organic social context, the contingency of the symbolic power on the originary drives of 'being' to consume. Constitutes what is hysteridentical to the extent that being a consumer has come to partly operate as a means with which organic formative strategies are based and the collective psyche of the cultural dispensation being based on ambiguous notions of the didactic.

The manner in which the consumer and consumer ethic can be characterized as hysteridentical in the cultural dispensation is through the facility of the 'initio' being 'present'/present in one cultural context and 'absent'/absent in another simultaneously. The discursive implications of the 'initio' penetrate the originary psychological drives through their capacity to concretize power in the jurisdiction of the 'being' in order to be cognizant of the benefits of his or her relationship with the master archetype that discursive training accords. The fact of purchasing or even the cultural facility of the fleunuer operate as the primary drives in the context of advanced modernity and it is their ambiguous location and their operation to incite originary formative and universal formative strategies that concretize their presence/ 'presence' across social and multi-cultural categories in the context of advanced modernity.

Hysteridence advances the psychological implications in relating to Baudrillard's notion of simulation, in that it is through the location of the psyche in the organic social context that one's 'initio' or lack of 'initio' is purported to demonstrate social background and his comprehension of the 'signs' or 'codes' that comprise his social and cultural background. While simulation explicates their differentiation, hysteridence demonstrates the measure with which even the values of consumers from different social backgrounds have the same ethics and ethos regarding social and cultural hierarchy, comprehension of the operation of knowledge and the logocentric logic operating with epistemic implications.

> *"It is this combination of rationales for differentiation that institute systems of signs whereby different aspects or quantities of 'knowledge', 'possessions' or 'high culture' can define our status and relative grouping(p 54;68)."* (Hegarty; 2004, p 20).

In that at the heart of consumption in both art and utilitarian products, a measure of the teleological operates with a unifying implication, that this discourse designates as hysteridentical. The 'rationale' that Hergarty explicates in the context of modernity is related to the teleological amassing of wealth and how it is a logic that can break the aporetic borders between communities for example.

Art practice and the 'initio'

Art practice is significant in that it is informed by a measure of production that subsumes the originary 'initio' with its implication for individual creativity and operations outside the confining auspices of the symbolic power. It is also consistent with Jung's notion of the art being informed by a higher perception than the personal connotations of discursive training or personal art (Jung; 1966). The ethics of consumption in the context of art practice are also informed by this hysteridentical bridge between 'high culture' and 'low culture', where the point of purchase and consumption are not contingent on the cultural background of the consumer but on the ethics and ethos of universal consumption.

Hysteridence seeks to demonstrate that these lines between high and low culture are organically blurred, based on the contingency of the discursive training from the symbolic power that disseminates different social pathos and ethos but with an epistemic and collective goal. The differentiation is enabled by the propensity of the discursive training to rely on 'being' drives as mechanisms for auto-references in order to concertize the extent to which accretion and the epistemic can justify disparate ethos and cultural. The hyper-individuality that the 'initio' enables, with the immediacy of the historic and epistemic implications in the context of the ablative exercises being relevant in the structure of the 'initio' as a didactic facility in order to institute a substitution. It becomes imperative to establish a neutral context upon which the ablative exercises where 'performed' as being imbued with an ambiguity that is about what is epistemic about power in order to concretize what is logocentric. This way they could be discoursed as universal and supplementary.

Gayatri Spivak's notion about the manner in which these ablative exercises sought to institute a neutral universal cultural context where limited not only by the implications of logocentrism and its Eurocentric perspective and manner of recording them.

It was also influenced "by the way in which writing in general has provided a rhetorical structure to justify imperial expansion" (Morton; 2003, p19) "Gayatri Chakravorty Spivak"

Morton further explains that this model of the logocentric is that "one of the main problems with this transparent model of language is that it has been previously used to represent and constitute the world as a stable object of western knowledge" (2003; p 18). The manner in which it has influenced the structure of 'signs' and the metaphoric connotations of the symbolic power, the universal has been imbued with a differentiation mechanism that became contingent on organic processes in the community being concretize as lacking agency through lack of the discursive training.

Chapter 9

Art, the "Negative" and Hysteridence

In this chapter the discourse will demonstrate the necessity that is incumbent on the symbolic power to conceive of an 'image' of 'itself'. It will demonstrate the measure with which the 'image' seeks to concretize the 'absence' of 'negative' that informs and structures the measure with which the symbolic power establishes a relationship with the community.

The discourse also has to demonstrate how the community is concretized as metaphoric of 'absence' and the symbolic power is concretized as metaphoric of 'presence'.

In this chapter the discourse has to demonstrate the measure with which it is only the symbolic power that has implications for both 'absence' and 'presence'. That this is the only way it can attempt to account for the fullest of presence and establish a relationship with the supplement. The discourse will also demonstrate how the symbolic power accounts for the fullest measure of presence through operating as a maternal or germination facility in the cultural dispensation.

It will incorporate Kristeva's (in Lui) notion of the pleasure principle in the processes of mastering social interactions and contexts. That this principle in the context of modernity is necessitated by the propensity of the 'being' to exhibit his or her agency or organic jurisdiction. That even though this concretizes the measure with which 'being' cannot account for the fullest measure of presence, 'being' has the originary facility to defer towards it.

The discourse will demonstrate that 'being' is imbued with an originary agency by incorporating Lyotard's (in Malpas: 2003) notion of 'signs of history'. The discourse will demonstrate that this notion has relevance in art practice's transcendental connotations. That it also concretizes the notion of hysteridence has relevance for both the community and the symbolic power. That art also makes history without making grandiose historical statements, the discourse also demonstrate how even the symbolic power makes history without making grandiose historical statements, that is what it characterizes as hysteridentical.

The chapter will also seek to demonstrate the measure with which the community has had to merge with the context of modernity in an ontological or psychological extent. It will demonstrate through art practice, that the fragmented processes of the symbolic power are concretized, where the 'absence' that characterizes the community has relevance for the conscious and the unconscious.

It will also demonstrate the measure with which this 'absence' is symbolic, and how this is the only manner in which 'signs' in the context of the community are imbued with metonymic connotations and implications.

Of Art and Hysteridence

Since the negative aspect in the context of supplement operates with a measure of the metonymic, it can also subsume the gestation and germination that is connoted is formless or without structure. In that not only does it necessitate the cultural formation to conceive of an 'image' for itself in relation to the supplement, in order to auto-reference and to reference to the facility of the initium or the enunciative field that permeates the image of the cultural formulation.

In the context of the supplement the split between the 'absence' and presence or 'presence' is detected through the 'sign' or the tool, a measure that instigates the metonymic operation but also imbues the location of 'absence' with a 'negativity' or non witnessable aspect that is symbolic or metaphysical when it is deferred towards. It also concretizes the ambiguity of the 'sign' in 'being' and that it is imbued with didactic connotations. The split between 'absence' and presence is through the certainty of presence being able to account and differentiate itself from itself and other aspects. The split is necessary in that not only does language imbue 'being' with an ambiguous operation of self-presence through the symbolic presence of language, but it is also that which requires teleological justification of and through language and 'being' to justify his cultural formulation.

The discourse seeks to demonstrate that when it refers to the 'negative' in relation to the supplement, it relates to that which cannot be witnessed in a temporal measure, and that which can be symbolically deferred towards in the intellectual and cerebral processes of 'being'. The notion of splitting is symbolic of the 'absence' and its symbolic connotations that operate the measure of the metonymic in the operation of the 'sign'. It is also symbolic of the 'presence' that concretizes the cultural formulation as a didactic facility that has relevance to the symbolic relevance of the supplement or 'absence'.

The notion of the cultural formulation being an image of an aspect of the supplement, connotes that which is intangible and palpable about the relationship between the cultural formulation and the supplement. In that desire for the didactic in the context of the cultural formulation is deferred to temporal deferral when it is pragmatic and to the metaphysical when it is related to the supplement. The measure of the supplement can also be related to 'negative' or maternal symbolic function, in that not only is it imbued with the ambiguity or the simultaneous operation of a 'presence' and 'absence', but it becomes paramount to place the supplement parallel to the conscious and unconscious, in that both can be detected to be imbued with an ambiguity of a presence and an 'absence'.

The key to the cultural formulation is that it institutes this split between the 'absence' and the 'presence', in that not only does the 'absence' connote a 'negative' or is it unwitnessable. In order to concretize its symbolic aspect or operation it has to assume metonymic operations or that which can instigate a context where a substitution can be possible. In that a substitution can exhibit that the 'sign' is inherently imbued with a measure of divisibility that concretizes the metonymic operation in the 'sign'. That this divisibility can exhibit that there is already and always 'negativity' or unwitnessable that can be 'represented' or deferred towards in the of the structure of the 'sign', in that not only is it symbolic, it is also that which has implications for that which is to come.

If we compare the symbolic operation of the maternal to the supplement, it also connotes that which is 'absent' or that which does not have a 'voice', and that it is cognizant of its symbolic operation through the auto-reference that its ambiguous structure affords it. That which instigates desire is not the moment of inception, and it cannot be said that it is the moment of previous residual experience in the context of the supplement and the establishing of a relationship with the cultural formulation. Rather this is the context in which the metonymic operation instigates a substitution through the presence of 'being' and the symbolic operation of language. It's not that the moment of instigation is arbitrary, rather it is consistent with the 'repetition' of 'absence' or 'non-interaction' between 'being' and the supplement. This can only be discoursed through the fact that 'being' is cognizant of desire instigating debate about the fullest measure of presence, that the 'sign' or language instigates this split, between 'absence' and 'presence' and that not only does 'presence' require the tool or 'sign' to be imbued with evidence that it is auto-referential. It also requires that an 'other' be 'present' or present, for the purposes of juxtaposition and illumination that can imbue a context with connotations for which is to come that has implications and connotations for the trace.

This measure of the substitution also applies in the maternal function or 'negative' aspect of the supplement. That not only does the phallic fantasy image operate to concretize desire in the location and operation of the instigator but it also renders the 'negative' function or maternal function as auto-referential and imbued with an ambiguous structure. In that the maternal function is imbued with the ambiguous measure of being witnessable and not being witnessable through the positivist operation. This is the measure with which the phallic fantasy operates in a metaphoric sense, in that even in the context of the supplement the relationship can be established through the 'stimulation' or instigated by desire, to use the erotic image. This way 'absence' is not just symbolic but it is metonymic in its operation and imbues 'being' and an 'other' with a common 'absence' they are both conscious of. The 'absence' or desire for the didactic in 'being' and the 'absence' of the unwitnessable in the maternal or 'negative' function.

When the negative or the supplement is 'stimulated' it is also that which can be imbued with a measure of substitution in the context of establishing a relationship with the cultural formulation. In that not only does the 'sign' or language place 'being' in a position for auto-referencing but it also marks that point where 'being' has been cognizant of the imminent substitution through desire and repetition. That in the context of 'being', in order for 'being' to not reference towards a void in the context of his relationship with the supplement, he has to be conscious of desire as a stimulator of the substitution. In the context of the initial relationship with the supplement it had to be characterized by a repletion and repetition of desire and what is instinctive about desire or that which is 'absent' about the ontological implications in the operations of accretion and substitution. In that in order for the supplement to be detected to operate as an accretion and substitution facility, even at the context of establishing a relationship with the supplement, 'being' is already always cognizant of the discourse of the fullest measure of presence. Since the cultural formulation cannot account for the fullest measure of presence, the initial encounter between 'being' and the supplement was characterized by accretion through the repetition of desire and the substitution through the originary symbolic function of 'being' in relation to 'signs' and the 'absence' of the supplement.

The context of the initial encounter with the supplement does not exclude 'being' not interacting with 'signs' or tools prior to this relationship, its that the tool and the language had not transcended the context of accretion in the initium or the enunciative field. Rather the appropriation of the fullest measure of presence imbued the didactic desire with metaphysical connotations and imbued the 'sign' a propensity to auto-reference. Since the 'sign' cannot operate beyond temporal deferral and spatial differing, it is in the symbolic and metonymic operation of the cerebral space of 'being' that the 'sign' assumes transcendental connotations.

In the context of the substitution from rural and feudal context into modernity, the measure of accretion that informs the epistemic, was also characterized by an 'absence', that the substitution was already always gestating in the various cultural and economic dispensations prior to it. The 'phallus fantasy' in the context of gestation and germination assumes an auto-referential 'presence' that is comprised through deferral by 'being' but also a 'presence' that is unrepresentable in the social context but only in a symbolic measure that is informed by desire for what is didactic. Also through accretion in the context of the initium or the enunciative field, and by the immediacy that marks the separation and establishing of the modernity context.

The notion of the phallus fantasy applies in the context of the substitution from rural and feudal context to the context of modernity, in that the symbolic power subsumes epistemic implications and connotations that are implicitly about the collective unconscious where implications of desire for the didactic and the mastering of that which connotes this desire informs the symbolic operation the symbolic power. It is a symbolic operation that subsumes that a measure of 'presence' the image of the fantasy phallus applies in the context modernity. In that not only does the image of the phallus subsume creativity and progress, it also subsumes a measure of infinite deferral that the measure of 'absence' in relation to establishing a culture formulation and desire in relation to the supplement, also requires deferral to this 'absence' through mastering its implications.

In that in the context of modernity the measure of the immediate social transaction, a measure of the 'new' encounter is connoted and it is imbued with a binary structure, where an essentialism in the
structure of the 'sign' can be detected to imbue the context with 'birthing' a formative education. That is about instruction and the intuitive implications of being imbued with an 'absence' in the context of the community or individual without the facility of the 'initio'.

That the 'being' who lacks the facility of the 'initio' is consistent with the 'absence' that connotes the supplement, he or she is not parallel to it, in that he or she is constantly referring to the 'absence' that it is informed by a structure that inculcates it. This 'absence' has already always been in incorporated in the unconscious drives of 'being' and has been incorporated in the conscious drives in the context of modernity in order for 'presence' or presence to be imbued with a measure of positivism. This is also the measure with which 'signs' in the social contexts are 'being' 'born' through the conscious and unconscious drives. In that the negative is that whose structure is informed by what is 'absent', parallel to the context of the supplement where that which is negative also operates as an auto-reference that allows it to be imbued with its own representational aspect. In that the negative in the context of the supplement characterizes the fullest measure of presence and the referral that is connoted thereof. In the context of the relationship with the symbolic power, this relationship is imbued with an image that is not just about 'presence' but also accommodates the image of the phallus fantasy. In that if the supplement can be conceived as symbolic of the maternal and the symbolic implications of gestation, then modernity can be characterized as being the produce that characterizes the measure of accretion and germination from the rural and feudal context.

In that if the supplement is characterized and informed by its own representational aspect, then in the context of modernity the measure with which the location of 'absence' the relationship between 'being' or community and the symbolic power, is primarily informed by the drives of the metaphoric and metonymic that in modernity are contingent on the didactic inculcation of the symbolic power. Where the symbolic power inculcates itself as the 'master' of the gestation and transformational manifestations in the context of the substitution from the rural to the context of modernity.

Art practice can exhibit that the symbolic power can be characterized as a 'splitting' facility or a 'birthing' facility into the context of modernity. Since art practice in the context of modernity has to be imbued with temporal and spatial differing connotations in its structure, it is also that which exhibits that it does not refute the teleological and didactic operation of the symbolic power. It concretizes that the discourse of the exegetic is primarily a didactic discourse in the context of the symbolic power to demonstrate that it is imbued with a relationship with the supplement.

In that the temporal context in which 'signs' operate in cannot subdue the operation of desire for the didactic, and that this can be exhibited by the symbolic power inculcating that the social context is characterized by an 'absence'. This 'absence' also exhibits that 'being' has an originary relationship with the supplement that is about justifying the representational aspect in the supplement 'being' auto-referential and that 'being' desiring the didactic in the context of modernity is characterized by the divisibility of 'being', being informed by the context, the 'presence' of desire for the didactic and the significance of the social context being illuminating unto itself and to the 'being' who occupy it. In that when the context is illuminating unto itself then the phallus fantasy image applies where the symbolic power can still be conceived to 'master' the gestation and germination and the product of the substitution.

Art practice does not refute the propensity of the symbolic power to 'master' the substitution, rather it examines the didactic and formative implications of 'absence' that in the conscious operation of the 'being' are deemed to be 'barren' of didactic connotations and implications or are that which operate in an overt negative or aggressive measure. That this has implications for the measure with which what is didactic in the structure of 'signs' can establish a relationship with 'signs' through 'being' drives.

The negative function in the context of the supplement also has to be imbued with a splitting mechanism that enables it to auto-reference, in that the cultural formulation is cognizant of it operating as a 'natural' or natural facility. The cultural formulation receives its teleological implications from this facility, but since the supplement is also imbued with a gestation or negative function, with its own condensation and displacement facility that enable deferral towards a cultural formulation. This internal process in the supplement also enables 'being' to defer to the fullest measure of presence, in that not only does the fullest measure of presence defer to the presence in the temporal, but it also refers to the infinite 'absence' that comprise its structure.

This infinite 'absence' is not only a negative aspect in the supplement, but the image of the fantasy phallus also applies to it in the sense that it can exhibit that processes of gestation are not static or dormant, but are consistent with the 'absence' that characterizes the location of the 'being' and the community in the context of modernity. Where social transactions are characterized as 'new' or informed by a measure of creativity on both 'being' imbued with the facility of the 'initio' and 'being' is who is 'barren'.

A deconstruction reading and analysis of the social context can exhibit the measure with which the 'absence' is also imbued with an ambiguity that is about splitting from the germination operation that traditional social training engenders and encompasses. That presence is not necessarily about this 'presence' but it is about exhibiting the teleological implications of the symbolic power and the symbolic implications of 'splitting' from the rural to the urban context. That the symbolic power has inculcated the traditional social training its processes to be that which is imbued with this negative or germination, that is about the 'presence' of the symbolic power and the 'absence' of the community. Where the 'absence' of the community imbues the facility of the substitution from the rural to modernity to be informed by a teleological operation that subsumes what is epistemic and a relationship with the supplement that is imbued with originary connotations.

In the pleasure Principle Kristeval also incorporates the notion of the 'pleasure principle' that is imbedded in the context of gestation and germination processes. This discourse seeks to inculcate that this pleasure principle is not imbedded in the structure of the social training, but is rather imbedded in the originary processes of 'being' and the collective community. In that the ontological implications of this pleasure principle are that which are 'present' in the context of 'being' and comprise that which Kristeva characterizes as 'unrepresentable' in the context of the relationship between 'being' and the symbolic power. That the structure of 'signs' that are inculcated and disseminated by the symbolic power operated in a measure that is isolated and essentialist. That the symbolic power is characterized to be informed by the structure of 'signs' that operates independently of the supplement in order to demonstrate their logocentric logic.

The supplement/supplementary, hysteridence and 'signs of history'

In the processes of supplementary gestation and germination the measure with which 'signs' are 'present'/present has precedents over the aspect which governs them or operates as a condensation facility. By this the discourse means they can be characterized as having an hysteridentical relationship with the condensation facility. In the context of the symbolic power, this relationship is contingent on the deferral propensities of 'signs' through their lack of the 'initio' of agency. This way power becomes a facility which passes down or demonstrates a devolution from the apex of the symbolic power. It is also the means with which the symbolic power establish and concretizes a binary or dichotomous relationship with 'signs'.

The facility of the 'initio' or 'agency as didactic or formative is a facility that operates with relinquishing implications in the context of the social interaction. Prior to the social context it is a facility in 'being' that marks the historic and metaphysical fact of the ablative exercises during the context of substitutions. It is contingent on the epistemic implications and connotations of the initium, and it is evidence of presence in the cognitive space of 'being' in terms of a phenomenology where what is exhaustible is paramount in the structure of the 'sign' and in the concretization the logic of logocentrism.

Hysteridence exposes a limitation in the notion of a phenomenology of exhaustion, in that through the image or the conception of the fullest measure of presence, the 'presence' of 'absence' in the structure of the 'initio' is concretized as a condensation facility. It has to be disseminated as 'negative' or 'absent' in order to establish the difference between the rural context and the urban context after the advent of the ablative exercise.

Art practice is able to demonstrate that the 'negative' aspect in the structure of 'signs' in the context of modernity enables 'signs' to concretize their relationship with the 'absence' of the supplement. It is a social context in which the organic originary creativity of the cultural dispensation manifests. It manifests by demonstrating and articulating the various condensation and metonymic facilities in the context of modernity that enable cultural diversity, the symbolic implications of economic activities like the transference of the 'signs' of value from rural to urban context for example and their historic or epistemic connotations.

Lyotard speaks of historic events as "signs of history" as explicated by Malpas (2003). 'Signs' of history are not limited to instances of political upheaval, rather they can also be extended to the symbolic and regulative roles of economic activities, like the arbitrary operation of 'signs' in the context of art practice. The context of art practice is contingent on the accretion of 'signs' for example and its symbolic operation as the social space where what is metaphysical and pragmatic coalesce. The notion of hysteridence seeks to demonstrate the measure with which the Kantian notion of 'history' and 'progress' (Malpas, 2003; 81), is contingent on the conception of identity as that which interrogates psychological implications in the organic social processes being 'conceived' or constructed in the deferral propensities of the discursive formulations and training. Demonstrates the extent to which agency can be concretized as originary. This way it concretizes the distance or institutes notions of progress from the rural context prior to the ablative exercises. It also enables the discourse that questions the essentialist of 'being' and the location of the community in relation to the symbolic power teleological.

The discourse of acknowledgments and distinctions seeks to demonstrate that art practice is an example of the Lyotard notion of a 'sign of history', in that it also interrogates the immediate social and cultural implication of a collective condensation facility, and the measure with which individual identity relates to both the symbolic power and his or her immediate social context.

Art and 'signs of history'

Art interrogates the essentialist discourse of the symbolic power both from a personal and political perspective. Lyotard's notion of 'signs of history' enable a conception of history as whole as art practice does without making grandiose statements:

> "*are less about progress and humanity's 'moral disposition' than they are signs of a collapse of organizing frameworks that represent themselves as universal. In fact each sign becomes for Lyo-*

tard a point at which conceptual and rational
ways of organizing history are called into ques-
tion and new ways of thinking (new genres of dis-
course) have the potential to emerge" (Malpas,
2003, 83)

The discourse of acknowledgments and distinctions purports that
the notion of hysteridence seeks to demonstrate that there are various condensation facilities in the social context that enable the
sublimation between 'being' and 'signs'. It seeks to demonstrate
that condensation facilities are not limited to the central govern-
ment, but they extend to the organization strategies disseminated
in the cultural dispensation, through the 'absence' that informs
'signs' and the devolution of power through the system, similarities
and consistencies in the ethos and pathos of the cultural dispensation
can be discerned to operate as 'signs of history' in communal and individual contexts. It is also that which provides a "distinction between
concepts" (Malpas: 2003), in the make-up of the symbolic power, in its
attempt to compensate for the fullest measure of presence.

Hysteridence is also the means with which 'signs' operate in a
measure where they defer to the fullest measure of presence, this
they achieve through their relationship with the supplement. Since
the 'negative' and the supplement are characterized by an 'absence',
the symbolic power's strategies can demonstrate the extent to
which contexts can be exhausted in the cultural dispensation.
Where they can be demonstrated to be examples of an adequation
with oneself or an undivided subjectivity between 'being' and the
'initio'.

Art practice with its propensity to operate from the annals of the
initium or the enunciative field in the cultural dispensation, is able to
concretize the measure with which 'signs' are imbued with an independence. This independence can demonstrate that the relationship
with the supplement is immediate to 'signs' and that this is only possible when the context is conceived through infinite referral.

It is only through art practice that society as an image of the supplement is able to demonstrate the measure with the fullest measure
of presence cannot be fully contained. Malpas (2003) explicates Lyotard's notion that the "role of art is to disturb or disrupt consensus
and to make possible the emergence of new forms and voices that
increase the range of possible ways to phrase experience" (p. 88).

The symbolic power is a facility that relies on its ability to auto-reference itself, in relation to itself, this way it is able to demonstrate the measure with which it is different from the rural context, and discourse the fullest measure of presence. The community in its passive location in the relationship provides a metonymic facility for the condensation facility that is the symbolic power, but the necessary variety in condensation facilities eschews the creativity that is inherent in the organic interactions in the community. It does this by rendering the metonymic operation of 'signs' barren of the sublimation facility that is inherent and necessary in the conception of a 'sign' structure as being informed by an 'absence' and 'presence' simultaneously.

Since the symbolic power is able to auto-reference itself, it is able to account for an image of the fullest measure of presence that has a relationship with the supplement, by deferring its metaphysical implications through itself as a portion or a supplementary aspect and in relation to spirituality or the exegtic in order to justify the logic of logocentrism. Hysteridence and the discourse of acknowledgements and distinctions provides a facility upon which history can be demonstrated to be 'played out' by the individuals and community that are contingent on the symbolic power for didactic strategies and implications. The discourse recognizes the distance between a condensation facility and its metonymic facility, in the context of advanced capitalism the community is not inferred in the formulation processes of the symbolic power or condensation facility. Since it also relies on an 'absence' in the structure of the 'sign' through its originary relationship with the supplement, it is a primary 'sign of history' in the cultural dispensation, but accounting for the fullest measure of presence without the facility of the supplement eschews creativity or sublimation in the operation of 'signs'.

Chapter 10

The Substitution and Art Movements

In this chapter the discourse will elaborate on the measure with which structures of signification are imbued with both 'negative' and positive implications in the context of the substitution and after the substitution. By also incorporating Mbembe(2001) notion of the postcolony, the discourse will demonstrate how positive and 'negative' signification facilities in the context of modernity are imbued with a logical history and discontinuities characterized primarily by the context of colonization or the substitution.

It will discourse the notion of the phallic fantasy in the operation of the maternal or germination operations of the symbolic power demonstrate the measure with which creativity or the masculine aspect can be related to the community.

Did for example the 'value' of wealth become concretized as symbolic even in the context of the individualistic context of modernity? If it did how come the structures of signification are characterized by an inconsistency in relating towards the supplement in the relationship between the symbolic power and community?

The discourse will demonstrate through the example of the structures of signification in the conception of wealth in modernity, that the shift from a symbolic conception of wealth and its collective connotations to an individualistic paradigm is also informed by the deconstructionist notion of a trace.

By also comparing the structures of relating towards the supplement between archaic Man and modernity. It will demonstrate in archaic Man 'being' related to the supplement through the repletion and symbolic operation of the 'sign' or tool. In the context of modernity the ablative exercise during the context of the substation or colonization, concretized a semiotic severance between the community and the supplement. The community then became primarily contingent on the cultural formulation to establish a relationship with the supplement.

The discourse will also seek to demonstrate that through this logic, the symbolic power came to establish the maternal function of its physical structures and processes. That this way the symbolic power can auto-reference and subject 'being' to its processes.

Citing Malpas (2003) who explicates Lyotard's notion of 'the differend', it can be demonstrated that the measure with which the community is unable to give witness has connotations for the discourse of origins in the context of modernity. The discourse will demonstrate that art practice is also able to demonstrate that this propensity has didactic implications that can be due to the diversity that characterizes modernity and the symbolic power instituting and inculcating this propensity through the strategy of 'absence' in the structure of the 'sign' of the community.

Of Substitutions and art movements

In the context of modernity, the community is cognizant of its implication towards the symbolic power as being imbued with a semiotic operation that is incumbent upon it to exhibit the metonymic and metaphoric implications of the didactic ethic. Since the didactic ethic is characterized by a measure of 'absence', and the 'being' is conscious of his or her 'presence' or presence in the context of modernity as part of psychosomatic and originary implications that what is didactic has connotations for accretion and the epistemic. In order for a 'sign' to be concretized as a metaphoric it cannot relinquish its metonymic or accrued significations, in terms of that which is epistemic and in terms of that which is didactic, but the context can be imbued with an 'absence'. In the context of modernity the didactic is imbued with a measure of 'absence' that the symbolic operation of the 'negative' or maternal has inculcated to have immediate and transient connotations and implications. In the context of archaic man, the didactic bases was founded upon the measure of the infinite or fullest measure of presence in relation to the supplement, this way it was contingent on the presence or 'presence' of 'being' as a symbolic didactic facility or entity. It was also due to the overt accumulative or accretion implications that the context was characterized in relation between desire for the didactic and establishing the structure of a 'sign'.

In the context of modernity the didactic is contingent on the 'negative' or the maternal function to operate as that which is the teleological vehicle for didactic connotations. That this is not only a facility for concretizing the essentialism of a 'sign' but it is also a supplementary facility that can demonstrate how the symbolic power is imbued with universal maternal or 'negative' didactic implications that concretize the metaphoric operation of the submissive location in the binary structure between the community and the symbolic power, it also concretizes metaphoric operation of the dominant location in the binary.

In the context of the substitution, in order for the symbolic power to exhibit a split from the previous paradigm, there had to be witnessable ablative exercises that the community could appropriate in an ontological measure, in order to establish existential relationships with the 'new' paradigm. These exercises established the subjectivity of 'lack' or 'absence', whose metaphoric and metonymic implications became embroiled in the teleological processes and what is supplementary about the symbolic power. The symbolic power in the context of the substitution can also be detected to function as a maternal or 'negative' image, in that not only does it confer the context of modernity with transformational inclinations and processes, but it also exhibits the processes and aspects within the symbolic power itself that induce a semiotic operation or transformational propensities.

In the context of the substitution the phallic fantasy image can be applied to metonymic or transformational implications of signification in the didactic implications and connotations of the economic 'being'. That there was   a shift from the ontological implications being invested in what is symbolic and collective about wealth into a paradigm that is individualistic and isolated from collective consciousness. That the metaphoric connotations where transformed by the logocentric logic to a positivistic presence in the context of modernity, a semiotic and supplementary operation that can be related to the unconscious through the maternal function of the symbolic power inducing a desire that is universal in the context of the substitution began to be inculcated.

The subsequent didactic strategies and implications where inculcated with fragmented implications, in that what is existential became concretized as a primary didactic and orientation facility. It also came to occupy the submissive location in the binary relationship with the symbolic power. In that through the semiotic exchange between what is ontological and didactic, the submissive location in the structure of the binary became concretized as metaphoric or condensation facility in modernity. In order to exhibit the measure with which what is creative and auto-referential as an example of mastering its own processes, the symbolic power imbued it with 'negative' or submissive connotations. That this became the didactic strategy for implicating towards the symbolic power, through an isolated and individuated implication.

The discourse has sought to demonstrate that the symbolic power in the context of modernity operates with the condensation aspect in the structure of 'signs', and that this enables it to concretize the discourse of 'presence' or presence to that which is witnessable and the propensity of the 'sign' to operate with its own jurisdiction. The discourse also maintains that the measure with which this dichotomy in the cultural dispensation is contingent on the immediacy of the social transaction or context concretizes the influence of the mastering processes of the symbolic power. In order for the symbolic power to demonstrate that it masters its processes 'signs' have to operate with metaphoric or condensation structures. That this can be detected in the semiotic processes in the context of the substitution, where the role of wealth for example was imbued with communal ethics and a heterogeneity that could be imbued with a relationship with the supplement that is informed by the heterogeneity that could imbued it with an exigency that exhibited how the supplement was imbued with its own representational aspect.

If we go back to the aspect of the economic ethics with symbolic and communal ethics, it can be detected that what was supplementary about the wealth was how it justified the presence or 'presence' of the cultural formulation as a didactic principle whose creativity or semiotic implications relied on the conception of the fullest measure of presence or the supplement. That there was an exigency that imbued the cultural formulation with a measure of creativity that was induced by the semiotic implications of desire and the mastering of the cultural formulation's processes.

In the context of modernity this exigency is incumbent on the symbolic power, in that not only is it related to the immediacy with which didactic strategies and ethics were required and disseminated in the context of the substitution, but it also characterized the measure of what is unrepresentable in the structure of an essentialist 'sign'. That this is also the extent to which 'absence' in the context of modernity is imbued with a measure of the didactic. In that in order for 'being' to implicate towards the symbolic power, he or she has to be cognizant and conscious of this 'absence' as being that submissive end of the binary relationship with the symbolic power.

As the discourse has sought to exhibit that art practice in the context of modernity examines the measure to which the 'negative' aspect is perceived and inculcated as combative, aggressive and antagonistic. That in the context of art 'signs' are able with their semiotic and transformational facility, examine the structure of 'absence' within its own internal processes. That this not only engages 'being' and the 'sign' in the processes of discoursing and mastering his or her own ontological processes in the context of 'being' and the 'signs' own unrepresentable connotations in terms what has been accrued by the 'sign' but it examines the notion of the substitution and its implications for splitting from the rural or feudal context. That in the context of the substitution the notion of the fullest measure of presence became imbued with the necessary 'negative' connotations and implications. This was the case in order for the symbolic power to experiment with the 'absence' as the foundational didactic connotations, and that in the context of the substitution desire was induced by the relinquishing of the previous dispensation and the measure with which 'being' required a universal or collective didactic ethic or strategies for orientation in the 'new' context.

Psychoanalysis has sought to demonstrate that when it comes to didactic and formative strategies, the subject or 'being' has to experiment with 'presence' in order to come to terms of mastering his or her ontological processes in the context of an adult or his or her relationship with the maternal figure in the context of an infant. In comparison to an infant the measure with which what is metaphoric about the maternal is fundamental to aspects of ontological and existential expression in a particular context, in the context of modernity the substitution can be compared to an infant's fragmented experience prior to the mirror stage.

Art movements in the early twentieth century, can be characterized as social and cultural paradigms in the context of the substitution into modernity, that even though industrialization and the ethics of individuality had been entrenched. In that the global community as an ethic was still fragmented not just due to the effects and affects of colonization but also due to the existential disparity induced by the homogenous narratives in urban settings and structures of the symbolic power. This can be exemplified by the institutionalization of capitalist enterprises that in the context of the colony split communities from their communal and rural cultural enclaves, into the urban and disparate individualist social ethics in the context of modernity.

This is the context that Mbembe (2001) characterizes as an "age (that) is meant not a simple category of time but a number of relationships and configuration of events often visible and perceptible, sometimes diffused, hydra-headed but to which contemporaries could testify since very aware of them. As an age the postcolony encloses multiple durees made up of discontinuities, reversals, inertias, and swings that overlay one another, interpenetrate one another, and envelope another: an 'entanglement'" (2001:14).

Substitutions as hysteridentical

In the context of western community entrenched and concretized the measure with which the existential effects were detected to influence the ontological beyond the measure of identity that discourses the economic 'being' and the multi-cultural for example. This age included the cultural 'being' who was conscious of the cultural eclecticism that capitalism is defined by and was contingent on to concretize the measure with which didactic universal ethics are 'absent' in the global cultural dispensation, this it could disseminate the epistemic as comprised of an historic 'inertia'. That these epistemic inertial and discontinuities are also the measure with which the community occupies the submissive location in the binary relationship with the symbolic power. Therefore the context of the substitution can be deemed to be characterized by what is hysteridentical by these entanglements, where in the context of modernity came to operate as foundation of divisive ethic and the homogenous narratives in the urban context where the emphasized fragmentation.

That the fragmented nature of the cultural dispensation could be detected in art movements, where not only did one particular movement focus on a particular social or cultural issue. For example Dadaism was a reactionary movement to the world war one conscription around Western Europe, a period in the history of modernity when the 'negative' aspect in the logocentric logic was being inculcated with overt violent strategies. This is a period in which applies the Deconstructionist notion of 'negation' or revealing the secret in the cultural dispensation between the 'denial' of what is positive and creative about the logic of 'presence' of the symbolic power and the revealing of the jurisdiction of the 'initio' in the context of symbolic power.

In that this period in the history of modernity marked the measure with which the symbolic power had to demonstrate or exhibit the measure with which the 'absence' that is 'barren' in the cultural dispensation and the measure with which what is 'negative' is consistent with the exhaustion that social transactions are inculcated to be structured by in the context of modernity. Plus the measure with which they are indivisible from 'being' who is imbued with the facility of the 'initio'. This could be detected in the measure with which soldiers interacted and still interact with civilians, and the measure with which the logic of hierarchy could and still exhibit the extent to which 'presence' is symbolic when it operates 'independently' from the supplement. Since 'absence' cannot be separated from the supplement it becomes embroiled in the discourse of originality and authenticity that in the context of modernity has been pronounced by the discourse of representation, both what is 'representable' and that which is 'unrepresentable'.

In that in the early stages of advanced modernity it could be detected that cultural identity came to subsume economic ethics when what is 'unrepresenstable' in an existential measure was pronounced by the encounter with an 'other', or that which is epistemic in the context of an 'other' and the symbolic power.

That through the social training the symbolic power exhibits the measure of ontological and existential auto-negation, in that not only does 'being' identity have to be separate from the rural and feudal context, but it also has to be imbued with a 'secret' that is about implication to the symbolic power, that concretizes the 'presence' or presence of the symbolic power. In the context of the art movements this 'secret' becomes revealed through the discourse the relationship with 'signs' that still maintains a measure of the epistemic and the originary. This way what is ontological can be detected to implicate towards the symbolic power through the 'secret'. Art practice's teleological operation in the context of modernity can be detected to be imbued with a discourse to 'reveal' this 'secret', in that not only does the epistemic and originary relationship with 'signs' enable the 'sign' its 'own' partition as the Deconstructionist inculcates, but this partition can be detected to be induced by the experiment with 'presence' in the context of the substitution into modernity where it has severed a relationship with the rural and feudal context.

That according to the operation of the maternal metaphor can be demonstrated to be imbued with a measure of the transformational that has an originary relationship with the supplement through incorporating the epistemic operation of the 'sign'. That this can be detected in the operation of the 'signs' when in its essentialism can be exhibited to also rely on the initium or the enunciative field or communication or exchange of 'signs'. When it operates it exhibits the measure with which it is supplementary and contingent on that which is beyond its structure or through deferral to that which is beyond its structure. That its signification does not cease to be imbued with an essentialism, but this essentialism can be examined or questioned when it can be detected to induce auto-referential propensities in an attempt to deny identity both for that which is contemporary and for that which has epistemic connotations. In that when it has epistemic and originary connotations identity operates with and in the submissive location in the structure of the binary with the symbolic power and when it is imbued with contemporary connotations it operates with the essentialism of 'presence' or presence according to the logic of logocentrism.

The 'Initio' as Logocentric

The notion of hysteridence can demonstrate the measure with which Lyotard's notion of 'the differend' has implications in the didactic and formative strategies in the context of modernity. Where the essentialism of the 'sign' concretized the manner in which deferral is about auto-negation when 'being' implicates towards the symbolic power, and is about power in a context where the 'initio' becomes discoursed.

The facility of the 'initio' for example emanates from these didactic strategies in the context of modernity, if traced in the context of the ablative exercises where and when substitutions characterized the development of modernity. It can be demonstrated to be a facility that eschews the originary jurisdiction that cultural formulations in the rural context imbued 'being' with. As the initial metonymic facility in the context of the substitution in the context of the substitution, it was also the means with which 'absence' was concretized as part of the structure of 'signs' according to logocentric logic.

This way one could implicate towards the symbolic power while being cognizant that the discursive training does not inform the didactic and formative connotations of the initium or the enunciative field that the symbolic power is contingent upon for 'signs'. The jurisdiction of the 'initio' is also able to operate as a metonymic facility by sublimating the location of the originary jurisdiction or agency in 'being' from the rural context, this way what is supplementary about the symbolic power and the rural context can be concretized to justify the teleological implications of the symbolic power.

It has to be stated that the initium does not influence the operations of the discursive and the symbolic power, in that they both require formulation both to demonstrate a relationship with the supplement and concretize this sense of 'absence' in the context of the community and in the formative implications of 'being' that have to be inculcated with the facility of the 'initio'. This shows 'the differend' is able to thrive in a social context in which, the appropriation of the didactic implications in the symbolic power render the 'being' silent or barren of an agency cannot only concretize their role in the formulation of the symbolic power, but also demonstrates how the symbolic power has a metaphysical role and position.

In the social context hysteridence emanates from acceptance that the 'absence' in the structure of 'signs', by establishing in the context of the substitution, that accretion and the epistemic become mechanisms in the context of the symbolic power to demonstrate the 'presence'/presence of power or jurisdiction in its repertoire. The differend becomes apparent when this power can be related to the supplement, not only to concretize the measure with which it is 'absolute' but also to exhibit the measure with which it cannot be deferred towards in a measure that questions this 'absolute'. In that not only can this jurisdiction abjure the 'being' who possess the 'initio', but it also abjures his or her originary relationship to the symbolic power or the 'initio' he or she possess.

Malpas characterizes the differend in the following manner and how it enables engagement of 'the differend':

> "The differend, the site of conflict where one or more of the opposing parties is condemned to silence, calls for testimony. It is not a question of resolving a differend according some set of pre-established rules. Instead the existence of the conflict that engenders it must be brought to light and new means of bearing witness be sought" (2003; 89)

Hysteridence is able to 'the differend' by discerning the instability in the didactic structures of 'signs' as that which abnegates the agency of 'being' as both a possessor of the 'initio' and the one who implicates towards it. This state of affairs does not enable 'being' to be a witness to their implication even though there are ontological and didactic benefits to it. Since hysteridence emphasizes both negative and positive aspects of implicating towards the symbolic power, it demonstrates that the 'absence' in the structure of the 'sign' operates with metonymic implications and connotations in order for the hierarchies and strategies of subordination in the cultural dispensation to operate with transformative or sublimation implications. This way their 'pure' or 'essentialist' structure can be demonstrated to only be transformative in the processes of formulation in the context of the symbolic power.

Hysteridence seeks to demonstrate that when the metonymic connotations are positive, or witnessable when they have implications for the context during the social interaction or have implications for 'presence'/presence and when they are negative they simply concretize the negativity. Since 'being' already always emanates from the stand-point of 'absence', their presence can be deferred towards a phenomenology of exhaustion since it can be demonstrated that they are barren of the discursive training.

Hysteridence seeks to demonstrates these are the contexts upon which the measure of negative didactic strategies in the social context can develop, in that according to the didactic logic of the symbolic power, the 'negativity' concretizes this distance between the symbolic power and the community.

The community is cognizant of hierarchies for example, that they cannot operate or be in place without their participation, since drives operate through metonymic implications, it is the measure of the social encounter that is a primary indicator that they are in place. Since the assumption is already in place that they are susceptible to instability in the context of the community, what is hysteridentical emerges in the organic processes of the community to justify the teleological relevance of the 'negativity' by adopting the 'negative'/negative relinquishing strategies of the 'initio'.

Woodard (http://www.iep.utm.edu/lyotard/#H5) explicates Lyotard's understanding of the limitations of reason and how that impacts representation:

> *"Lyotard introduces a distinction between opposition and difference to account for the differing ways in which the discursive and the figural function. Difference corresponds to figure, and the distinction between discourse and figure it-*

self is said to be one of difference rather than op-position. In opposition, two terms are rigidly op-posed and quite distinct; in difference, the two terms are mutually implicated, yet ultimately ir-reconcilable."

The discursive can be detected to have a condensation role in this discourse and the figural a metonymic role, the 'absence' that characterizes the location of the community in the context of the symbolic power can be demonstrated to emanate and dependent on the symbolic power. That this extends beyond the social context, it is also relevant for the existential processes, where hierarchies are concretized immediate to the logic of 'absence' or the negative, where what is hysteridentical can emanate from the comprehension and acceptance of the didactic location. Where what is metonymic is concretized as a sublimation facility in order to implicate towards the symbolic power.

The discourse seeks to demonstrate how in the social context it is the figural that has a primary operation, where deferral and implication are indicators for associating with the symbolic power. What is hysteridentical emerges out of being conscious of the condensation structure of 'signs', where it becomes reasonable to appropriate the 'absence' or 'absence' as primary didactic facilities.

Chapter 11

Hysteridence, Art, the Substitution and Signification

In this chapter the discourse will demonstrate the extent to which structures of signification are contingent on the measure with which the 'signifier' has to have the same source or emanate from the same cultural formulation. It will demonstrate that the formulation has necessitated that 'signs' be imbued with a positivistic and positive structure in the processes of the symbolic power and 'negative' in the context of the community.

The discourse will also demonstrate the measure with which performance art does not have teleological implications in the context and processes of the symbolic power.

It will demonstrate how the signification processes in the processes of the symbolic power enable what is hysteridentical between the community and the symbolic power to thrive. That the artist will always be conscious and discourse the 'signifier' that defines his or her passive location in relation to the symbolic power.

The discourse will also interrogate how signifying concretizes the dichotomous relationship between the community and the symbolic power, between modernity and the context before the substitution or colonization. It will demonstrate how hysteridence organically develops in the context of the community in order for 'being' and the community to account for how they implicate towards the symbolic power.

The discourse will demonstrate how what is hysteridentical can be detected in the structure of the 'initio' as a condensation facility. How this facility is the only didactic or formative facility that 'signifies' in the social context between 'being'. That this is the only context in which the 'distance' between the community and symbolic power is concretized and deemed 'present'.

In this chapter the discourse will also demonstrate the measure with which performance art can operate as a 'sign of history'. How as a sign of history performance art instigates metonymic structures more than condensation structures in the social context.

Of hysteridence and signification

The 'signifier' develops as a result of repetition in the social context. This can be also detected or gleaned in the context of archaic Man, where the 'sign' even as an abstract didactic facility relied on a didactic narrative to disseminate itself in the fabric of the cultural dispensation. Desire can then be characterized as that which imbues 'signification', the 'signifier' and the 'sign' with a measure or structure of the supplementary. In that not only does desire help instigate a relationship with the supplement, it also provides 'being' and the context of the unconscious with a facility for reunion with the logic of the supplement through their articulation of their teleological implications.

The ethic of 'absence' in the context of modernity and its symbolic processes through the essentialist structure of the 'sign', emphasizes the 'presence' or presence of the symbolic power. Whose symbolic relationship to the supplement can be traced through the epistemic and what is accrued in the ambiguity of the initium or the enunciative field. The ethic of 'absence' and what is didactic about it, relies on the auto-affection or the symbolic location or operation of 'being' for the 'presence' of the symbolic power through auto-implication. It became significant in the context of the substitution for the epistemic to be essentialist in structure in order to concretize the measure with which presence of the symbolic power can be foundational on the contingency of 'accident' that informs the relationship between 'being', the community and the logic of the binary structure. This way that which is affective will defer towards an 'other' in that originary measure that concretizes the cultural formulation as symbolic instead of the location of 'being'.

That the contingency of the 'accident' that informs the structure of the essentialist 'sign' can be detected to inform the 'absence' in the context of 'being' and the community in modernity. It is that space where cultural origins can be questioned and the administrative processes of the symbolic power can engage the discourse of homogenous narratives in the urban context for example. Since the community becomes embroiled in this discourse, this is also the measure with which that which is hysteridentical emerges, that location where the community is conscious that it participates of being 'barren' of orientation facilities in the context of modernity.

That also through the historic encounter with an 'other' the discourse of origins is informed by the immediacy and transience that concretizes a 'complication' that is accounted for in the contingency of the 'accident'.

This measure of the 'accident' and 'complication' becomes pronounced in the context of the community, in that not only does the 'lack' or 'absence' concretize itself, but the operation of the drives and desire imbue the ontological with that which is originary. That in the essentialist implication of modernity occupy what is oppositional or deteriorated in the structure of the symbolic power. In the context of the substitution or the realization of the split from the maternal symbolic connotations of the originary rural culture, through the originary facility of the initium or the enunciative field 'signs' maintained their epistemic and accrued signification, with the effect of structuring the essentialism or binary structure of the symbolic power.

The symbolic power also had to exhibit the measure with which it was informed by a split from the rural and feudal structure of 'signs', the measure with which it could achieve this was through instigating a reunion with the maternal or 'hidden' operations and relationship with the facility of the supplement. Through the epistemic and accretion it was that which exhibited positivist or witnessable strategies and ethics of its didactic implications, with the emphasis on desire and drives through renewed economic and political ethics.

What is hysteridentical emerges through the accretion and repletion of these didactic contingencies of 'accident', 'complication' and 'deterioration' that informed the encounter between 'other' in the urban context. In that what is hyseridentical is informed by what is positive and overt in terms of the operation of didactic principles, but it is also an ontological and teleological result of appropriating the 'negative' and 'hidden' didactic principles. Hysteridence is also a result of the ambiguous socially organic spontaneity that the transience and immediacy of the social context imbues and concretizes the measure of the present or 'present' and 'negative' or negative. The discourse is seeking to inculcate that the 'being' and the community have to be conscious of that which is hysteridentical in order to exhibit the measure with which repletion and repetition in the transient social context inform the logic of presence. That the community is conscious of the measure with which the operation of the binary in the binary structure, what is positivist precedes that which is 'hidden', or what is positive precedes what is negative.

That in an ontological measure the extent to which 'being' is symbolic of the presence of the symbolic power, he or she through implicating 'negates' a measure of identity which through auto-affection desires a relationship with the symbolic power but it instigates a 'negative' relationship with the symbolic power through the submissive location of 'being'.

The Maternal Image and Art

The maternal image in relation to art practice anchors the measure with which 'signs' are epistemic through their deferral to the symbolic power. In that not only is what is affective also informed by that which is positive in an ontological sense, it is also positive in terms of the didactic implications through seeking a 'balance' with the symbolic power. In the context of modernity this 'balance' or the measure with which art practice instigates a reunion with the symbolic power is through the 'nothingness' notion that in the Dadaist movement was consistent with the didactic 'absence' that informed the social and cultural context. That the artists in the movement were conscious of the didactic implications in the social context, but this is also the measure with which the 'signs' and their essentialism in the context of modernity have to be extracted or split from their epistemic relationship with the symbolic power in order for 'being' to exhibit the extent to which he or she has an affective relationship with them. In that it is in the context of art practice 'being' can exhibit that desire provides a structural facility for 'being' and what is didactic in the relationship with the symbolic power. That it through psychosomatic drives that induce 'being' to concretize a relationship with the cultural formulation 'independent' of 'signs'. Since it is drive that also instigates 'being' being conscious of the submissive location and the teleological implications behind reactionary discourse. That the measure with which 'being' is imbued with agency is contingent on being conscious that 'signs' operate with their own agency, that allows them to be auto-referential and exhibit the measure with which they are supplementary.

The discourse seeks to exhibit that what is hysteridentical has ontological connotations, in that not only is what is didactic in the context of modernity imbued with a measure of 'absence'. This 'absence' extends to the 'jurisdiction' of the 'sign' or the implement, in that not only is the essentialism that informs its didactic implications, but it also concretizes the measure with which 'being' occupies a symbolic location in the relation to the cultural formulation and its didactic implications.

The 'nothingness' in the themes of Dadaism was contingent on the essentialist 'jurisdiction' of the 'sign', in that if the art piece was symbolic or comprised of 'nothing', it was due to its essentialist connotations inherited from the didactic strategies and ethics in the symbolic power as 'barren' of the measure of the universal both in the context of the unconscious and the positivist social transaction. Not only were these art themes consistent with the immediacy and transience that characterizes the context of modernity, they were and are consistent with the structure of the social transaction being exhaustible, where as the art work is exhausted through the momentary performance or the viewing in the exhibition, the social transaction is exhaustible through the immediacy structure of the social transaction. The discourse is not stating that social transactions are choreographed, rather they are contingent on repetition as that which concretizes its teleological and didactic connotations in the 'being' whose jurisdiction is imbued with the facility of the 'initio'.

The organic agency of the 'being' who is barren of the facility of the 'initio' is informed by the contemporary initium or enunciative field, in that not only is the community symbolic of the connotations with which the submissive location occupies the relationship with the symbolic power, it is also that which enables the organic transaction to be 'independent' of the symbolic power. That in the social context between transactions of the community, desire concretizes the submissive location as the 'signifier' with which it negotiates social orientation, since it is contingent on the heterogeneous implication in the relationship with the symbolic power, the submissive 'signifier' assumes and concretizes the 'negative' structure it is informed by. It also concretizes the measure with which what is symbolic about the 'dominant' in the ontological processes plays the ambiguous role of concretizing the didactic role of the 'initio' and the submissive role of the 'being' who is 'barren' of it. That the 'dominant' role or the 'initio' in the didactic connotations of the symbolic power instigates the drives of 'being' in terms of desire concretizing his or her organic jurisdiction.

That the measure with which 'being' orientates the ontological is through the essentialism of the 'negative' didactic implications of the symbolic power, through which it can demonstrate the 'negativity' or 'absence' of didactic connotations in the context of the community. That this is also the extent to which 'being' becomes a symbolic facility of the didactic implementations of the cultural formulation, not only does this realize the measure of 'lack' that informs the ontological processes of 'being' in the context of modernity, but it also provides the didactic orientation facility.

That the 'negative' aspect in the context of modernity assumes metonymic connotations when that which is epistemic is imbued and informs the 'signifier' in the context of the symbolic power. Since the metaphoric operation is pronounced or has been imbued with essentialist connotations, it never questions or impedes the heterogeneous and autocratic implications and connotations of 'signs' in the context of the symbolic power. When Kristeva states that the subject of desire that emerges is realized through drives, she means that in the processes of auto-affection 'being' is not informed by an 'inner-conflict', rather it is the ethic of auto-negation that informs the facility of the 'initio' as that which concretizes the symbolic operation of 'being' and concretize the teleological implications of the symbolic power. That a necessary measure of dissimulation is required in order for the operation of the ethic of 'absence' or the 'negative' to be imbued with didactic connotations, that it is this dissimulation that pronounces the existential and ontological as isolated from the community and the symbolic power. That it imbues the location of 'being' in the structure of the 'sign' and its didactic connotations as that which is already always 'revealed', in that in order for a didactic operation to be operational it has to enable auto-differentiation in 'being' and the measure of the 'sign' to be ambiguous.

What is hysteridentical emerges out of the organic processes of the community and the conscious relationship with the contemporary didactic operations of 'signs', it forms part of the subject of desire and its instigation of that which is didactic through existential and ontological processes. It is that location where 'being' is conscious and cognizant of the measure to which he or she is a symbolic facility in the cultural formulation, and it is also the measure with which the symbolic power exhibits its necessary essentialist structure in the context of modernity.

Hysteridence can also be characterized as the measure with which 'being' and the community develop a 'signifier', the location where signification or 'meaning' of the 'negative' and its didactic connotations 'reveal' his or her implication towards the symbolic power.

The significance of the discourse incorporating art is that art production also subsumes the facility of the drives, art is also a manifestation of the psychosomatic orders in 'being', in that when Kristeva states that desire induces 'being' to live at the expense of his or her drives, she is stating the measure with which the 'absence' in the context of modernity is symbolic of the supplementary operation in the processes of the symbolic power. In that the 'absence' imbues the context of modernity with an 'aid' for the substitution from the originary rural and feudal structures and notions of didactic conceptions. In the context after the substitution 'being' drives have had to be implicated towards the symbolic power instead of a supplementary operation in the structure of the 'sign'.

Hysteridence in the context of modernity is imbued with the ambiguity of that which operates as a supplementary, in that not only does it exhibit the extent to which the community is 'barren' of the didactic implications of the symbolic power, it is also that which concretizes the measure of the 'absence', in that the 'absence' that informs it also informs the 'absence' that informs the didactic implication in the strategies of the symbolic power. The 'absence' of that which is hysteridentical can be characterized as that which is unrepresentable in the structure of 'signs' in modernity, that it is consistent with the notion in the rural and feudal context of that which was unrepresentable in the operation in the context of the 'other'. This could be detected through the facility of the initium, where the 'other' operated as part of the processes of language and deferral, as both a 'sign' that is about concretizing the auto-deferral and auto-referential processes of 'signs' in the particular cultural formulation.

That which is supplementary has connotations for 'signification' that seek to reunite language with the 'body' or the psychosomatic orders and processes. This way the ethic and strategy of 'absence' (or that which is 'negative' in the didactic conceptions that operate with 'being' conscious) drive and subsume the context of the substitution while being cognizant of the epistemic and accretion. It can be demonstrated that both are contingent on the drives for a measure of both dissimulation and overt implication towards the symbolic power, in the context of the substitution.

In the context of modernity language emanates from the symbolic power's operations, not from the supplement or the facility of the fullest measure of presence, rather it is informed by the fragmented structure of the symbolic power and its metaphoric institutions. This enables the symbolic power to inculcate itself in a measure that essentializes 'signs' and extracts language from the body and to an extent from the operations of the unconscious in order to concretize the structure of immediacy to be informed by that which is witnessable or positivist. This way what is teleological about the symbolic power can be exhibited to be informed by ontological processes and the facility of the supplement through the facility of accretion and the epistemic.

Art practice in the context of modernity is an attempt at this reconciliation between 'being' and language. In that even if the reconciliation is attempted through the visual language it discourses that which is affective and the measure with which the context of the substitution characterized a split from the rural context not only induces discourse of the pleasure principle, but also the pleasure of agency and the realization of a didactic and orientation facility.

In the context of modernity the pleasure principle has to experimented with through reunion with the collective consciousness, that accounts for the extent to which the separation concretized 'being' as an essentialist symbolic facility under the auspices of the symbolic power. That art practice can exhibit the extent to which auto-negation constitutes the masochism that an essentialist structure in the 'sign' concretizes 'being' as a 'sign'. That art practice is the rediscovering of, the pleasure of reunifying with the maternal image, where 'signs' are not essentialist or static, but rather operate with the metonymic implications of accretion.

Hysteridence, the Metonym and the 'Initio'

The notion of hysteridence can demonstrate the measure with which the 'signifier' in the social context is contingent on metonymic or replacements propensities. That this is consistent with the deconstructionist notion of infinite referral, where the logic of the dichotomy between 'being' who is barren of the facility of the 'initio' and the 'being' who posses the 'initio', the strategy of relinquishing differs when one is characterized by exhaustion and repetition. The lack of 'initio' in the context of community operates with the infinite referral of the differance. Power does not become interchangeable in the social context, rather the metaphoric operation in the 'possession' of the 'being' with the 'initio' renders it interchangeable in the logic of logocentric choreography that characterize the teleological and supplementary connotations of the symbolic power.

Hysteridence is able to demonstrate in the social context the measure with which the 'initio' is able to operate as a 'signifier' in a manner that concretizes that metonymic operations are fluid and contingent on the social context to exhibit their relationship to their condensation facility. The condensation facility is rendered 'absent' when it is deferred to the community, in the context where it is formulated, it subsumes the 'absence' of the supplement in order to defer its metaphysical and teleological implications in the social context.

In the context of the ablative exercises during the context of colonization, the 'sign' was assumed to be 'absent' or absent, not only did this concretize the distance between the community and the symbolic power, but it concretized a teleological operation, when it is teleological the 'absence' became inculcated as rigid as the 'presence' of the symbolic power.

The notion of 'the differend' is another critical theory concept that emphasizes the significance of 'signs' being able to defer perpetually, in relation to the notion of hysteridence they are both able to articulate how the social context operates with a measure of the historic without having to account for a grand narrative. Since social contexts require a measure of repetition, the accretion operates both with a measure of signification and a facility that Lyotard terms a 'sign of history'. Hysteridence operates as a sign of history by emphasizing the disparity and consistency between the 'absence' and 'presence' of didactic implications related to the inculcation of the 'initio' from the context of the ablative exercises and how the 'absence' in the context of the community was purported to be 'barren' of the teleological.

The immediate psychological and epistemic implications that hysteridence is able to demonstrate is that 'absence' cannot be deferred towards without being cognizant of the accretion that is implicated in the notion of the epistemic. The discursive itself as a formulation tool could not be imbued with deferral and referral connotations without incorporating the historic accretion of 'signs'. Hysteridence is a result of the propensities of the facility of the 'initio' to 'signify', where in the social context it is able to operate as a metonymic facility that is able to demonstrate the contingency of the 'absence' on the didactic in the social context of advanced modernity on the symbolic power and the submissive location of the community in the relationship. What is symbiotic about the 'presence'/presence and 'absence'/absence of the symbolic power is also in turn able to demonstrate how this 'absence' in the community becomes concretized. Hysteridence organically develops in the community in order to exhibit how it implicates towards the symbolic power, how this deferral is a product of a desire for the didactic than about rebellion. This is exhibited through the notion of hysteridence by how the condensation aspect that informs the 'initio' is able to 'signify' towards the 'absence' that was instituted in the context of the ablative exercises. This is how it demonstrates the distance that is symptomatic of the distance between the community and the symbolic power. That when community is 'signified' through the 'initio' there is an inevitability of recognition or realization of it's 'presence' not just as a condensation facility, but of how this condensation facility is contingent on the metonymic operation of the 'sign' of the community.

The metonym as a facility for cerebral implications is characterized by an ambiguity or a measure of the symbiotic operations, where the structure of a 'sign' as pure or essentialist does not apply. Rather what is emphasized in the operation of the metonym is the immediacy of the context, the mastery of the context through training and repetition, in the context of art the pronounced sublimation and creativity connotations. What is hysteridentical seeks to expose that this is the measure with which what is metaphysical is able to inform the 'sign', the 'being' and the accretion. That the condensation facility is contingent on are characterized by the 'breach' of communication which mostly emphasizes auto-reference in the social context and in the context of the symbolic power emphasizes the condensation facility, what is logocentric about it and what is metaphysical about it.

Performance art is another facility that is able to operate as a sign of history, in the sense that contexts are contracted and choreographed for a particular discourse, the context becomes extracted from history not for just interrogating the historic process. The personal and the political and their metonymic implications are pronounced through the significant role the body plays in the context of performance art. Since the location of the community in its relationship with the symbolic power is characterized by passivity, the notion of hysteridence seeks to demonstrate that the metonymic operations are that which seek to exhibit that the condensation facility is deferred towards through the devolution of power in the context of advanced community.

What is hysteridentical recognizes the fluidity and creativity that is subsumed by the metonymic facility, where it cannot be purely 'negative' or purely 'positive'. As a facility to master the social context, the metonymic enables social creativity, and that pronounced auto-referencing concretizes the breach of communication.

Chapter 12

Organized Sublimation and 'the real'

In this chapter the discourse will examine the notion of 'the real' or hyper-reality as that which has developed in the context of modernity from the structures of signification and their essentialist implications. That if 'signs' can operate as simulation then they are a result of the symbiotic ethics of social and cultural synthesis between communities deemed to be 'high' or 'low' culture.

The discourse will demonstrate by citing Singh (2003) through the notion of sublimation, 'being' and 'signs' are that which are in a conscious participation with the 'formulation' and concretization of 'the real' through the structures of signification in the cultural dispensation operating with overt fragmented implications.

It will explicate the difference between sublimation and cerebrinity. How the notion of sublimation relies on the structure of the 'sign' to be expanded, that in the context of the unconscious and conscious enables the 'being' to appropriate 'new' or 'alternative' definitions without didactic or formative connotations.

That what is cerebrinous has implications for recognition of didactic connotations and their propensity to illuminate the didactic necessity. That since sublimation instigates the transformational propensity of 'signs' through expanded boundaries, the notion of intellectual illumination concretizes by desire. It will demonstrate that through investing energy onto objects, or through 'cathexis' sublimation and cerebrity. That sublimation instigates the conceptual immensity in the structure of the 'sign' in the conscious and unconscious and cerebrinity enables conceptual reductionism.

The chapter will also demonstrate the relationship between creative drives and sublimation concretizes the relationship between conscious and the unconscious through referral propensity of the 'sign' in the conscious operation. How creative drives also influence the expansion and contraction of 'signs' in the unconscious, that this concretizes 'being' operation as a supplementary facility.

That 'being' supplementary operation can be detected through what the deconstructionist discourse designates as the breach of communication between 'being', the definition of objects and their concrete structures.

This chapter will demonstrate how in the context of modernity 'signs' and institutions have had to be fragmented in a measure that is pragmatic and concretizes the logic of logocentrism.

The discourse will demonstrate the inevitability of 'the real' or hyper-reality in the context of modernity. That the essentialism that informs the structure of 'signs' became the measure with which they relate but also the measure with which the symbolic power disseminates itself and informs the structure of 'signs'. That this is the measure with which the symbolic power operates as a feminine principle imbued with order and germination. The discourse will demonstrate how the exhaustable operation in the structure of the 'sign' concretizes its contingency on the symbolic power or the feminine principle.

Organized Sublimation and 'the real'

The significance of incorporating visual art practice in the oeuvre of critical theory, is that it is able to help discern the epistemic operation of 'signs' independent of the auspices of the symbolic power. The discourse of acknowledgements and distinctions examines the measure with which 'signs' in the context of advanced modernity operate with the measure of the 'signifier' instead of the operation of the 'sign'. The logic behind the notion of 'the real' or hyper-reality is a notion that is contingent on the measure with which 'signs' operate with the logic of logocentrism that 'signs' are cognizant on the cultural location in the context of advanced modernity.

With the discourse of acknowledgments and distinctions the logic of 'signs' is examined from their social impact, their psychological, cultural and didactic connotations. If 'signs' have become simulations of 'other' 'signs' this is demonstrative of the measure with which the notion and logic of 'absence' in the operation of the 'sign' has relevance for both 'low' and 'high' culture. That even in the context of the symbolic power and its discursive operations, the aspect of collective consciousness is imbued with an operation of 'simulation'. Where 'signs' are cognizant of epistemic implications, where the strategy of the 'boundary' in the operation of the 'sign' is pronounced and imbued with metaphysical connotations.

The discourse of acknowledgments and distinctions the notion of the boundary in the structure of the 'sign' can be detected to be imbued with referral propensities in the context of the collective unconscious. This is the context where the notion and facility of sublimation operates with the metaphysical connotations of the supplement and the supplementary. The quintessence of the 'sign' is concretized by the cerebrinous illumination in the collective conscious where it operates with essentialist connotations, that space where collective consciousness relates to 'signs' in terms of the conceptual immensity of the sublime and the unconscious. In the context of the sublime and unconscious the notion of boundary is expanded, vast, contained by the propensity to refer to the supplement, expanded by desire for the didactic operation in the structure of the 'sign'.

This context applies to the discourse of acknowledgements and distinctions to the extent that perception and conceptual recognition where sublimation is a facility that enables through temporal deferral the symbolic power to differentiate itself from itself, in a measure that relates to the ego by emphasizing development and growth in relation to 'signs'. This is the context in which 'being' and his ego have to establish didactic goals through discursive training or as in the context of modernity lack thereof. What is cerebrinous can demonstrate that a sublime experience emanates from the unconscious in a measure that is about recognition or instinctive familiarity, where desire meets realization. This is in a context where there is a lack of training leads to the 'alternative' didactic strategies or what the discourse of acknowledgements and distinctions designates as hysteridentical. That in the context of modernity the community is conscious of the measure with which the context is structured and defers to the rural context as oppositional to the symbolic power.

The significance of the notion of 'the real' is that since it inculcates that it is comprised of 'signs' that simulate other 'signs'. 'Signs' are that which in the context of the initium operates with the immensity of essentialism, where it has to be ambiguous in order to defer to it, and in order for it to concretize its structure. Critical theory has sought to demonstrate that in the structure of 'the real' the 'sign' is cognizant of the forces that operate and inform its structure. That its boundaries are contained and tenuous, only relevant to the particular context or are 'temporary' in a measure that influences their essentialism in the particular context. According to the discourse of acknowledgements and distinctions this is also what informs their sublimation.

In the context of sublimation and its relation to the notion of cerebrinity it is the expanding of boundary and limits of the 'sign' that eschew its quintessence, rather it becomes necessary to facilitate the measure with it becomes instinctively recognized, the process Singh explicates as:

> *"...during the experience we don't actually focus our eyes on the scene, and we thereby facilitate the production of alpha waves which are typically related to relaxation"* (2003; 14)

Relating to 'signs' in the context of 'the real' requires being conscious of the essentialism that separates organic contexts from conceptions of the symbolic power and its epistemic connotations. This also applies in the context of the unconscious in the space where the immensity that is instigated by the recognition requires the facilities of the Id in order to control the recognition and imbue it with a boundary. This way the processes of transformation that can be instigated in the context of the unconscious and the cerebral space can retain the residual epistemic structure of the 'sign', and when the 'sign' becomes instinctively recognized for its operational contemporary structure it induces reconciliation with the 'sign'. The processes of sublimation also instigate repletion in the cerebral space of 'being' similar to the reconciliation of the mirror phase, since the 'being' engages the fragmented processes of intellectual exercises, what becomes pronounced are the processes of temporal deferral and spatial differing which can concretize the measure with which consciousness directs individual goals like desire for the didactic and the development of the ego.

The notion of 'the real' can be detected to also instigate cerebrinous processes in that even when the recognition of simulation or play that transpires in the conscious mind and space can demonstrate the measure with which 'signs' have a supplementary aspect, this aspect enables 'being' to relinquish 'meaning' or to invest 'cathexis' (Singh; 2003) onto an object. The 'purpose'/purpose behind simulation is to reduce the repletion in the cerebral space when relating to the 'sign', in order for the ego to recognize the goal of 'play' or representation. This reduction can be related to how 'being' relates to temporal deferral, in that once the 'being' has reconciled the goals of 'play' in relation to 'signs', limitation oper-ates as both a facility that reduces the immensity of repletion and instinctive recognition in the cerebral space, it also operates as a means to instigate creative drives.

Creative drives pronounce the structure of the 'sign' as a referral facility in the context of consciousness, they also pronounce the immense repletion in the context of the essentialist unconscious and how it is necessary in the context of the unconscious for the 'sign' and 'being' to defer to the supplement, in order to facilitate the supplementary operation of play and individual creativity.

In the context of advanced modernity the immensity of the 'sign' has been reduced after the advent of the substitution, this has re-sulted in the measure of the didactic operation in its essentialist structure in the unconscious to be pronounced or has pronounced its supplementary implications. This supplementary reduction has also affected the measure of reconciliation in relation to the sym-bolic power.

In the context of the substitution, 'signs' 'reduced' structure insti-gated the transformational propensity of the 'sign', it also concre-tized the measure with which 'being' relates or establishes cathexis with the 'sign'. In that the 'absence' that structured the relationship with the symbolic power helps establish boundaries and limits in relation to 'signs' in the context of advanced modernity. It also con-cretized the measure with which the breach became pronounced as both a facility for the unconscious and a facility for consciousness when relating to 'signs'. Since 'signs' became reduced in their in-troductory immensity in consciousness, this enabled the symbolic power to operate as a feminine aspect that is both a repository for deferral, but also that which reduced the necessary immensity of the breach of communication between 'being' and 'signs'. The breach's necessity to be immense not only instigates alpha waves and precipitates conceptual recognition of the sublime, but it is also necessary for the immediate cerebrinous reconciliation between the supplementary operation of the 'sign' and its relationship with the supplement. It also concretizes the space in consciousness where 'signs' are facilitated by the Id or are instigated by the exter-nal influences of the 'initio' or the symbolic power.

When the 'breach's immensity is reduced, the facility of the boun-dary and the limit in the structure of the 'sign' becomes immediate, when it is immediate it becomes pronounced, when it is pro-nounced it becomes exhaustible in an immediate measure. Since even at the moment of 'inception' or initial interaction with the 'sign' the 'being' is informed by an 'absence', the breach is already always realized and exhausted, the 'sign', 'being' and the context are barren of a facility to juxtapose either as a didactic facility or as a mechanism for the development of the ego. The 'being' in relation to his or her ego is able to reduce the implications of the breach through instigating goals for the ego. This can be through ritual, or 'other' individuals who are examples of didactic implications in the community. The necessity to find goals for the ego continues the implication of the breach, it also renders originary relationship to the teleological connotations of the supplement.

What is hysteridentical develops in this lack of a facility to juxtapose both existential and cultural context in the cultural dispensation. It is also that which since the 'being' relies on cathexis, is able to imbue the 'absence' in 'being' with existential connotations. This way 'being' is also 'barren' of goals for both 'self' and the 'ego' in terms relating to 'signs' when initially encountering them and becomes contingent on the repository facility of the symbolic power and the discursive training for conceptual comprehension of 'signs'.

The notion of 'the real' is also significant to the extent that when 'being' desires, he or she is instinctively contingent on the repletion and breach of communication as immense in consciousness, in that not just as a learning facility, but they also dictate the capacity to comprehend temporal deferral and reconcile spatial differing. The contingency on the Id is also evidence of the necessity of the breach and its originary implications, it also pronounces the measure with which the symbolic power is a reduced 'sign' in order to be able to be differentiated from the context prior the substitution, the supplementary operations of the supplement, the immensity of the collective unconscious and the capacity of the context of the substitution to merge with the epistemic and logocentric logic.

What this discourse seeks to attest is that during the subliminal experience it is the 'sign' that becomes pronounced, the context becomes a reconciliation facility. In that it not only instigates the didactic and formative implications after the experience but it also concretizes the activity of instinctive drives. Since the notion of 'the real' is detected to be contingent on the essentialist structure of the 'sign', it is not contingent on the capacity of the 'sign' to merge with the previous context or previous structure. Rather what enables the 'sign' to be imbued with essentialist connotations is the measure with which it defers towards the supplement. This way its supplementary operations will emphasize the facility of the boundary that is consistent with the contemporary, epistemic and logocentric logic. The 'sign' in the context of advanced modernity is cognizant of its boundary's capacity to enable the context to be exhausted, in that in the context of modernity that which enables juxtaposition, since it is to come it can be evidenced is 'absent'.

The "Sign" as co-dependent

The notion of 'the real' emanates from the necessity in the context of modernity to define the pragmatism of the fragmented structure of the society, it articulates how the symbolic power also came be concretized and fragmented with independent operations from the community. As modernity developed, the 'sign' came to be concretized by how it auto-references, and emphasizes boundaries instead of the measure with which it defers both to the symbolic power and to the supplementary operations of the symbolic power.

The emphasis on boundaries also emphasized the capacity for the symbolic power to auto-reference and operate with organized structure of the feminine principle instead of the manifestation and creative implications of the masculine principle. Since the 'sign' also emphasizes the measure with which it auto-references it also cannot refer to the fullest measure of presence, rather it defers to the symbolic power as a didactic facility, pronounces the measure with which the 'absence' in its structure operates with the contextual emphasis of the exhaustible. This way it also operates with the manner in which deconstructionism states that it cannot juxtapose itself, since it does not refer to the fullest measure of presence, it cannot juxtapose to the previous context before the substitution.

The 'sign' cannot operate without its own supplementary measure this can be detected in its contingency on the epistemic and the logic of logocentrism. The essentialism of the 'sign' is also that which is concretized by the 'absence' that in the context of the substitution could be demonstrated by the 'absence' in the structure of the symbolic power. The 'sign' was inculcated as that which emanated from the symbolic power rather than the socially organic initium that informed the context before the substitution.

From a psycho-analyses perspective, 'being' relates to the 'sign' in a measure that is consistent with the repletion and expanded boundaries during the experience of a sublimation. This way 'being' is constantly having to interpret the manner in which the 'sign' operates, as if encountering or interacting with it for the first time.

In the context of modernity, since contexts are exhaustible, the 'sign' warrants interpretation to the extent that since it cannot be juxtaposed, its structure can collapse, the manner in which it defers, the manner in which it cannot defer to fullest of measure of presence, the manner in which it can only defer to the symbolic power through its logic of 'absence'. A 'sign' can collapse through auto-referencing, in that when it is interpreted its 'dependence' becomes pronounced, and how it is unable to offer 'being' with a deferral goal, but rather operates with the passivity of its 'power' that emanates from the devolution of power from the symbolic power.

When the discourse states that a 'sign' should have a deferral goal, it states that its structure should mimic or resemble how 'signs' in terms of accretion in the context of the symbolic power are depended on the production of the discursive. This way the manner in which it is exhaustible can be traced to the symbolic power, unlike the logic that the 'sign' is contingent on its 'absent' structure. So that when it auto-references what is epistemic can also be traced to the context of the substitution, as an institutional didactic facility.

A 'sign' lacks a deferral goal when it only defers to itself and to the context, as that which are comprised of expanded boundaries, and these boundaries articulate the measure with which the 'sign' came to be concretized as such. For example in the context of art practice, the 'sign' cannot be imbued with symbolic or transformational propensities if how it operates in the contemporary context can only defers to its own structure. For example if the notion of mind as a 'signifier' is only relevant in a passive measure in relation to didactic implications, then when it operates as a 'sign' as an independent quantifiable concept, it becomes contingent on the negative measure it acquired 'meaning'.

A 'sign' is imbued with a deferral goal when it can demonstrate its transformational propensities, and its measure to defer in the context also demonstrates that the 'absence' in its structure is an accretion facility, rather than being a passive and concrete facility.

For example in the context of the substitution, the historic connotations of the ablative exercise are that which the master of ceremonies was conscious are 'barren' of didactic and formative implications in the 'new' context. 'Signs' assumed a transformational aspect that was contingent on the symbolic power, 'signs' became 'barren' of the deferral goals they were imbued with in the sense that they were characterized by an 'absence' in their structure in relation to the symbolic power. How for example people required a 'travel document' to move between the city and the rural context, the document operated to concretized the rural and urban dichotomy in the initial context of the substitution. This emphasized the dichotomy between the production of the discursive and the socially organic initium, both in the context of substitutions and the originary cultural formulations.

The context of the substitution characterized the measure with which the notion of sublimation can be applied to a collective context. For example the strategy of the binary also compounds the repletion of the 'sign', both in relation to itself and in relation to an 'other'. The inevitable oppositional locations in the relationship between 'signs' also concretize the lack of referral that 'signs' in the comprehension of 'the real' operate with. Where they emphasize auto-referral and their operational boundaries.

Pronounced and concrete they enable the context to be exhausted, in that context requires the facilities of 'signs' and symbols to juxtapose it to other contexts. This can be detected in the measure with which in the context of modernity it became necessary for the urban context to be differentiated from the rural context. This strategy not only concretized how the symbolic power became concretized as a didactic facility, but it also concretized how 'signs' can be characterized by a trace in relation to the symbolic power and the context of the substitution.

The reason why the discourse of acknowledgements and distinctions argues about the repletion of the 'sign' in the cerebral context of 'being' is due to the necessary strategy of essentialising 'signs' that also characterizes a reduction of the fullest measure of presence in relation to the community or the 'sign'. A reduction of the fullest measure of presence is characterized by the extent to which 'signs' primarily operate as formative tools, instead of being cognizant of the facility of the trace that an epistemic conception can enable. Collective sublimation can also be detected to be that which characterized a reductionist operation of 'signs' in the sense that 'the real' is a conception that demonstrates that the compact nature of the symbolic power concretizes the logic of the binary between itself and the community.

The reductionist operation of the symbolic power enables a reconciliation between collective consciousness 'lacking' or being characterized by an 'absence' in relation to the metaphysical conception of logocentrism and how the supplement enables 'signs' to be traced to their epistemic conception but be relevant to the didactic implications of the symbolic power.

The discourse maintains that this was achieved in the context of the substitution, where the facility of the initium in the organic social contexts prior the substitution characterized the collective consciousness and collective unconscious as facilities for the discursive or the production of the discursive.

The context of the substitution can be detected to have instituted in the cerebral spaces of 'being' the relaxation of comprehensive and cognitive alpha waves. In that during the ablative exercise, the language was instructive in order to establish the passive and dominant locations that the symbolic power and the community occupy in the context of the substitution. This can be achieved through the instructive context being purported that it is not characterized by a breach of communication.

As modernity developed it can be detected what became crucial for the psychological implications of the community was a definition of the terms of realization of the gratification that inevitably comes with realizing a didactic desire. It can be discerned though that the 'free association' that was instituted in the context of the substitution has supplementary and universal connotations. These connotations related to the establishing of communities, identity and the discourse of origins in the context of the city could be related to the compounded and expanded 'sign' of the citizen on an individual level and the reductionist strategy to the notion of the community in relation to the 'sign' of the community.

In the context of art practice in the context of modernity the realization of the didactic principle can be detected through the anarchistic discourse that can characterize art discourse. In that anarchistic discourse can demonstrate the supplementary nature of the symbolic power, the supplementary operation of 'signs' in the context of the community, and the despotic operation of the symbolic power. Singh (2003) demonstrates during a sublimation experience, the freedom of the alpha waves does not only "free the energy for the associative thinking which leads to conceptual recognition" (2003: 14), but it also renders the operation of the 'sign' as that which can be demonstrated to be imbued with the logic of the boundary, limit and structure that the initial stages of the substitution were characterized by.

Bibliography

1. Reynolds, J. " Internet Encyclopedia of Philosophy". Accessed February 28, 2017. http://www.iep.utm.edu/derrida.
2. Gale, M. *Dada and Surrealism*. London: Plaidon, 1997.
3. Lui, C. "The Maternal Metaphor: Kristeva." The Maternal Metaphor: Kristeva. Accessed October 8, 2016. http://english.fju.edu.tw/lctd/asp/theory/theory_works/69/study.htm.
4. Woebcke, C. "The Astrology Reading of a Lifetime in a Fine Art Book". Mercury-Hermes-Trismegistus-Thoth. Accessed October 8, 2016.
   http://www.myastrologybook.com/Mercury-Hermes-Trismegistus-Thoth.htm.
5. Maragoni, M. *Julia Kristeva: Live Theory*. London: Contiuum, 2004.
6. De Ville, J. "Desire and Language in Derrida's 'Force of Law'". Accessed March 15, 2009.
   http://repository.uwc.ac.za/xmlui/bitstream/handle/10566/302/DeVilleForceofLaw2009.pdf?sequence=4
7. Dickerman, L., Powell III, A. and Lowry, G. *Dada*. Washington: Alfred Pacquement, 2005.
8. Jung, C.G. *The Collected Works: Volume Fifteen: The Spirit in Man, Art and Literature*. Edited by Sir Herbert Read, Michael Fordham and Gerhard Adler. London: Routledge and Kegan Paul, 1966.
9. Hill, J. *The Myths of Analyses*. New York: Harper Perennial, 1992.
10. Freud, S. *An Outline of Psychoanalysis*. Translated by Helena Ragg-Kirkby. London: Penguin Books, 2003.
11. Hegarty, P. *Jean Baudrillard: Live Theory*. London: Continuum, 2004.
12. Morton, S. *Gayatri Chakravorty Spivak*. London: Routledge, 2003.
13. Oliver, K. "Tracing the Signifier Behind the Scenes of Desire: Kristeva's Challenge to Lacan's Analyses". In *Cultural Semiosis: Tracing the Signifier*. Edited by H.J. Silverman. London: Psychology Press, 1998.
14. Malpas, S. *Jean-Franscois Lyotard*. London: Routledge, 2003.
15. Woodard, A. "Jean-Franscois Lyotard (1924-1998)" in "Internet Encyclopedia of Philosophy". Accessed September 29, 2016
   http://www.iep.utm.edu/lyotard/
16. Lippard, L. *Mixed Blessings: New Art in a Multicultural America*. New York: Pantheon: New York, 1990.

17. "Resistance Art", Contemporary African Art, http://www.contemporary-african-art.com/resistance-art.html.

18. "The Trojan Horse Massacre", South African History Online, http://www.sahistory.org.za/dated-event/trojan-horse-massacre.

19. Turner, V. *The Ritual Process: Structure and Anti-Structure*. New York: Aldine De Gruyter, 1969.

20. "The Art History: Modern Art Insight". Accessed November 10, 2016. http://www.theartstory.org/movement-dada.htm.

21. "Contemporary African Art". Accessed November 10, 2016. http://www.contemporary-african-art.com/resistance-art.html.

22. Little, D., November 10, 2016 (2:30 pm), "Critical Theory in the Frankfurt School". Posted on *Understanding Society*, March 30, 2013. http://understandingsociety.blogspot.co.za/2013/03/critical-theory-in-frankfurt-school.html.

23. "Qualitative Research Guidelines Project", Robert Wood Johnson Foundation. Accessed November 10, 2016. http://www.qualres.org/HomeCrit-3518.html.

24. Vasiliev, Z., "Notes on Stuart Hall, Encoding, Decoding". Posted on Zhenia Vasiliev Blog November 22 2015,. Accessed October 20, 2016. http://www.evasilev.com/blog/notes-on-stuart-hall-encoding-decoding.

25. Mbembe, A. *On the postcolony*. Los Angeles: University of California Press, 2001.

26. Foucualt, M. *The Archeology of Knowledge*. London: Routledge, 1969.

27. Singh, K. *Ideas in Psycho-analyses: Sublimation*. London: Totem Books, 2003.

Index

www.ingramcontent.com/pod-product-compliance
Lightning Source LLC
Chambersburg PA
CBHW071352280526
45787CB00001B/289